The Pitmen Painters

Lee Hall was born in Newcastle in 1966. He started
writing for radio in 1995, winning awards for *I Luv
You Jimmy Spud*, *Spoonface Steinberg* and *Blood Sugar*,
all of which made the journey to other media. His
screenplay for *Billy Elliot* was nominated for an Oscar
and was adapted into a multi-award-winning stage
musical. He has worked as writer-in-residence for Live
Theatre, Newcastle, and the Royal Shakespeare Company,
and has adapted many plays for the stage, including
Goldoni's *A Servant to Two Masters* (Young Vic/RSC),
Brecht's *Mr Puntila and His Man Matti* (Right Size/
Almeida) and Heijermans' *The Good Hope* (National
Theatre). He is currently working with Roger Waters
on a stage adaptation of *The Wall*.

also by Lee Hall from Faber

BILLY ELLIOT: THE SCREENPLAY

published by BBC Books

SPOONFACE STEINBERG AND OTHER PLAYS

published by Methuen

PLAYS: ONE
PLAYS: TWO
THE ADVENTURES OF PINOCCHIO
COOKING WITH ELVIS & BOLLOCKS
THE GOOD HOPE
A SERVANT TO TWO MASTERS

LEE HALL

The Pitmen Painters

inspired by the book by
William Feaver

faber and faber

First published in 2008
by Faber and Faber Limited
Bloomsbury House
74–77 Great Russell Street
London WC1B 3DA

Typeset by Country Setting, Kingsdown, Kent CT14 8ES
Printed in England by CPI Bookmarque, Croydon, Surrey

A CIP record for this book
is available from the British Library

ISBN 978-0-571-24227-6

4 6 8 10 9 7 5

To Mickey Kelly
who taught me about art

Introduction

The Pitmen Painters was given its premiere at Live Theatre, Newcastle, in September 2007. I have been associated with the company for many years, and it was a pleasure to work with a team of people who I mostly knew well and who had a strong reaction to the play's subject. Almost everyone in the North East has some connection to the mining industry, and this was certainly true of many of us in the rehearsal room; all of us were using our lives, like the pitmen in the play, to make art about the realities of the region.

But as much as this is a triumph partly won by people like the pitmen in the play, as a group I think we felt a sadness that the majority today are still excluded from what we do. Despite an occasional Damien Hirst or Tracey Emin, the art world remains disproportionately cluttered with the sons and daughters of the middle classes.

When I was growing up in the sixties and seventies, the first generation to benefit from the boldness of the Labour Government of 1945, especially in education, had come of age understanding that the arts were fundamental to a life fully lived. The roots of Live Theatre lie in this moment, when there was a huge urgency, an almost missionary zeal, to take art to 'deprived' communities. I was hooked by their efforts and drawn into a richly rewarding life. But like so many in my profession, I find those advances are now being reversed. The globalisation of capital, the monopolisation of the media, and the deregulation of TV have produced a situation where we get less culture but pay more for it. It's both a joke and a tragedy as the working classes who are denuded of political power and spiritual succour are excluded also from the system of culture so ravenously enjoyed by their exploiters.

So, as a riposte to the notion that 'dumbing down' is inevitable if market forces are left to their own devices, we have made our little play about the pitmen painters. In my mind they are not so much an anomaly but reflect a huge yearning within the working-class and Labour movements for access to the best things in life. Our pitmen were not content merely to observe but made art themselves, and I find them exemplary. If we see culture or high art as something separate, something just to contemplate, buy and sell, we are far from the notion of culture and art as it was experienced for millennia before the Industrial Revolution. Culture is for living, not commodification, and art should be about taking part. Real art is communal and active; it is not owned by anyone, but should be the intellectual and emotional air we breathe. The more people who take part, the richer it is, and for every person excluded the poorer we become.

Obviously we live in an age of huge creativity. The internet has revolutionised means of communication, but a sense of loss is also palpable. We see lives blighted by lack of understanding and whole swathes of people who are drip-fed ignorance. I suppose I wrote the play to remind myself that something really did get lost, or at least that an opportunity was missed; but to regret the atrophying of our cultural muscles is not necessarily nostalgic – for if there is something to remember, there is also something yet to be won.

Lee Hall
March 2008

Author's Notes

This is the second version of the play, although, by the time you read it, whatever is on stage may have been transformed yet again. Theatre is a living beast, and I've found all of my plays are constantly evolving. The cast made an unusually valuable contribution to the play as it developed and it would not have been possible without Bill Feaver, Max Roberts and George Stephenson.

The 'Gresford Hymn' was written by Robert Saint, a miner from Hebburn on Tyneside, to commemorate the mining disaster at Gresford Pit, Denbighshire, on 22 September 1934, when 266 men and boys lost their lives in a gas explosion. It has been played at every Durham Miners' Gala Day since 1936.

The **Pitmen Painters** was first presented at Live Theatre, Newcastle upon Tyne, on 20 September 2007. This production was revived at the same venue on 3 April 2008 and transferred to the Cottesloe auditorium of the National Theatre, London, in May 2008. The cast, in order of appearance, was as follows:

George Brown Deka Walmsley
Oliver Kilbourn Christopher Connel
Jimmy Floyd David Whitaker
Young Lad Brian Lonsdale
Harry Wilson Michael Hodgson
Robert Lyon Ian Kelly
Susan Parks Lisa McGrillis
Helen Sutherland Phillippa Wilson
Ben Nicholson Brian Lonsdale

Director Max Roberts
Set and Costume Design Gary McCann
Lighting Design Douglas Kuhrt
Video Design Shanaz Gulzar
Video Editor Laura Flynn
Sound Design Martin Hodgson
Costume Supervisor Lydia Hardiman
Costume Supervisor (Newcastle upon Tyne)
   Lou Duffy
Assistant Director (2007 production)
   Tess Denman-Cleaver
Stage Manager (2007 production) Andrina Baird
Stage Manager Paul Aziz
Deputy Stage Manager Kate McCheyne
Props Supervisor Simon Henderson
Technical Manager Dave Flynn
Technician Andy Ramsey
Production Manager Drummond Orr

'Gresford', the miners' hymn by Robert Saint, arranged by David Whitaker, performed by the Hetton Silver Band

Characters

George Brown
Oliver Kilbourn
Jimmy Floyd
Young Lad
Harry Wilson
Robert Lyon
Susan Parks
Helen Sutherland
Ben Nicholson

The action of the play takes place
in Ashington, Northumberland,
Newcastle upon Tyne, London
and Edinburgh between the years
1934 and 1947

THE PITMEN PAINTERS

Act One

Projection on the first screen:

THE PITMEN PAINTERS
BY LEE HALL

And on the second, a series of slides:

1934
1.2 MILLION MEN WORK IN THE PITS

AVERAGE SHIFT: TEN HOURS

AVERAGE TAKE-HOME PAY:
TWO POUNDS AND SIX SHILLINGS

George comes onstage and starts to set up chairs for the class. Oliver comes in.

George Oliver.

Oliver George.

   Jimmy comes in.

Alreet, Jimmy?

Jimmy No, I'm not alreet.

Oliver What's the matter?

Jimmy I've been wading about up to me chest in water all day.

Oliver Not C seam, again?

Jimmy I was lucky to get oot – half the shift's still down there, getting pumped oot.

George They want to get that seen to.

Jimmy What do you mean? You're the one who wants to get it seen to. You're the Union representative.

George Divvint start.

Jimmy Look, it's your job to sort this out.

George Listen, there's a time and a placc for everything. In case you hadn't noticed, I am currently serving as an official representative of the WEA. If it's pit business yer after, it'll have to wait till the morning. A tanner.

Jimmy This is absolutely ridiculous.

Enter a Young Lad.

George What are ye doing here?

Young Lad I've come for the class.

George Yer joking, aren't you – oot ye gan.

Young Lad What's wrong with me coming? I thought yer wer supposed to be encouraging people to learn things.

George Aye, Workers' Educational Association. Not Skiving Little Arseholes' Association. This is a place of serious learning – so bugger off.

Young Lad It's not my fault, man. There's a recession on.

George There'll be a recession on the back of yer heed in a minute.

Harry comes in.

Oliver Harry.

Young Lad Mr Wilson.

George I didn't think ye were coming.

Harry I wasn't ganna but I had to get out of the house, man. Wor lass is driving iz crackers.

Young Lad They've let is inti other classes.

George I don't care what anyone else does. This is a proper educational institution for pitmen.

Young Lad Ye let *him* in, he's not a miner.

George But he's a mechanic.

Young Lad No, he isn't, he works in a dentist's.

George Aye, well, he's a dental mechanic.

Oliver Leave the bairn alone.

Young Lad Howay, Uncle George, I'll sit at the back and keep quiet.

George OK, on a trial basis only. That's a tanner, then.

Young Lad A tanner!

George Self-improvement doesn't come cheap, ye knaa.

Young Lad I haven't got a tanner – I'm on the dole, man.

Harry Here, son. That's for me and the bairn.

Young Lad Thanks, Mr Wilson.

George You shouldn't encourage him.

Harry I divvint see why he should be penalised for the cyclical nature of capitalism.

Oliver and Jimmy give their money too, and George writes it in the book.

Well, I still say we should be deing Economics.

George Give it a rest, Harry, it was the only tutor we could get at short notice. So let's just give it a try.

Lyon comes in.

Lyon Hello.

George Can I help you?

Lyon I'm sorry. Is this Art Appreciation?

George I beg yer pardon.

Lyon Art. Appreciation.

George You're not from round here, are you?

Lyon No, I've come up from Newcastle.

George Newcastle?!

Lyon I'm here to teach the lesson.

George Ah, Professor Lyon. Yes, of course, why didn't you say so – come in, come in. We were expecting you a bit earlier.

Lyon Terribly sorry. The train was frightfully late. It took over two hours.

George Wey, just try to get on time in future. We're very punctual you know, we're miners.

Lyon I'm really terribly sorry.

George All right, all right, let's not make a song and dance about it. Looks like we're all here – so let's get crackin', Professor.

Lyon Yes, absolutely. But I'd better explain I'm not Professor Lyon.

George Are you sure?

Lyon Of course I'm sure.

George You're not Professor Lyon?

Lyon No.

George Well, who the bloody hell are you?

Lyon That's it, you see, I am Mr Lyon. But I'm not a professor.

George So you're not from the University, then.

Lyon No.

George Where the hell are you from?

Lyon Well, I teach at King's College.

George Not the University.

Lyon Well, no. But we're affiliated to Durham – so there's no actual professorship.

George I'll have to get on to Regional Office about this.

Oliver But ye de de art, divvint ye?

Lyon I beg your pardon?

Oliver Ye de de art, divvint ye?

Lyon I, em, terribly sorry I didn't quite catch that.

Oliver Ye de de art. De ye not?

Harry Do you teach art?

Lyon Oh yes, absolutely, yes.

George So you have got the requisite qualifications, then.

Lyon Of course. I'm a master of painting. I was at the Royal College – with Henry Moore, actually.

George Henry who?

Lyon Moore. We were both on a travel scholarship in Rome together.

George Look, I divvint care where you've been gallivanting as a student. I'm just interested that yer qualified for the job. We set very high standards. We're pitmen. Well, except him. He's a dentist.

Harry Dental mechanic.

George And him, who's unemployed. But he's only here on sufferance.

Lyon Well, I've been teaching Art History in one way or another for at least fifteen years.

George Well, look, I suppose we'll have to give you a go – but you realise I'm going to report this.

Lyon I'll do my level best.

Harry What's that?

Lyon Well, it's a projector.

George Projector. For God's sake. Nebody mentioned electrical equipment to me. We'd've had to book the Mechanics Hall for that kind of malarkey.

Jimmy There's ne 'lectricity in here, son.

Lyon But how am I going to show the slides?

George Aye, well, you should have thought aboot that before –

Harry Let's cancel the whole thing.

Jimmy Can't you just describe things?

Young Lad Why doesn't he put it through next door – at the Guides'?

George You can't do that.

Young Lad They've got an extension. Put it through there and plug it in next door. The brass band won't mind. Here.

The Young Lad plugs in the extension.

8

Lyon Thank you very much.

George Wait a minute – for a start we'd have to get written permission, and then there'd be the question of paying for the electricity. I'll turn a blind eye this time as long as nobody tells Brown Owl.

Lyon Thank – thank you very much. Perfect. Thank you. I thought we'd just start with a basic introduction. You know, run through a few of the Great Masters before moving on to the more contemporary issues.

Oliver puts the lights out. The lamp comes on. George is in the way.

Let's see. Titian.

Jimmy Bless you.

The slide is in the wrong way.

Young Lad It's upside doon.

Lyon Terribly sorry.

He rectifies it. George gets in the way.

Jimmy (*to George*) Oot the road, man.

Lyon Ah yes, now this is a very good example of what I want to explore in these session. The fundamental tension between the innovation of the artist and the tradition within which they are working.

Harry (*aside*) I telt ye we should've done Economics.

Lyon Here you see we have a painter working at the height of the Church's patronage, but as you can see at the very same time is obsession with pagan mythology – one of the grand themes of the Renaissance – (*He pronounces it 'Renissince'.*)

Jimmy The what?

9

Lyon The Renaissance.

Jimmy The Renissince?

Lyon Yes.

Jimmy The Renissince?

Lyon Well, the early Renaissance.

Jimmy What?

Lyon Oh, alrighty. The Renaissance. Anybody?

Nobody explains.

Raphael?

Nothing.

Leonardo?

Blank faces.

Leonardo da Vinci?

Jimmy Is he a painter?

Harry Of course he's a painter. Leonardo da Vinci – he's the most famous painter there is, man.

Jimmy Did he do that one of the cat?

George Course he didn't do the cat. That was Constable.

Lyon No. Constable is much later. Leonardo is perhaps the acme of the entire Renaissance.

Jimmy I thought you said he was a painter.

Lyon Yes. He is a painter.

Jimmy Well you've just said he was an acme?

Lyon No. The high point – the creative flowering of the entire Renaissance.

Harry Ah! The Renaissance. The Renaissance! He means the Renaissance!

They all laugh.

Lyon Yes, the Renaissance –

Harry Yes. Of course. It was after the Middle Ages, wasn't it?

Lyon Yes, from the fourteenth century to the end of the sixteeth. And . . .

He changes the slide to show the ceiling of the Sistine Chapel.

Perhaps the crowning achievement of the entire period, of course, is Michelangelo's Sistine Chapel. You have heard of the Sistine Chapel?

Jimmy Is that the one in Blaydon?

Lyon Where? No. Blaydon?! No, this is Rome. You do recognise these images don't you? *The Last Judgement*? *The Creation of Adam*.

George We haven't really seen much art, actually. That's why we hired you, like.

Harry To be quite honest with you – we were more keen on Introductory Economics, but we couldn't find a tutor.

Lyon May I ask you, have you ever been to a gallery?

George We've never been anywhere. We're pitmen.

Jimmy I went to South Shields once.

Harry And I fought in the Somme.

George Did you see any art?

Harry Of course I didn't. I was gassed, man.

George Aye, well shut up, then.

Lyon But surely you must have seen these images in books? (*Checks himself.*) From the library.

Oliver Library?

Lyon There's no library.

Oliver Harry's in the New Left Book Club – but they divvint gan in much for pictures. If yer not into leeks or whippets yer pretty much stuffed round here.

Lyon But you've never actually looked at a picture in real life?

George Well, no.

Lyon Well, I don't mean to be rude in any way, but may I ask – why have you chosen to do Art Appreciation?

Pause.

George To appreciate art.

Jimmy What's wrong with us wanting to appreciate art, like?

Lyon Nothing at all.

Oliver Most of wi left school when we were eleven, so there's a lot of things we divvint knaa – but that's why we come here – to find oot about the world.

George We're not thick, you know – well, apart from Jimmy. We just finished Evolutionary Biology.

Lyon Well – look – I think we should battle on.

He shows a slide.

Ah, yes, here we have a typical example of the Florence School – around 1560 – the relationship between the Cupid and the Virgin Mary is a standard tableau . . .

Harry 'Scuse me. Can I stop you a second?

Lyon Of course.

Harry I don't mean to be controversial, but I really don't think this is what we had in mind.

Lyon I'm sorry?

Harry Looking at paintings of cherubs and all that.

Lyon You don't want to look at paintings?

Harry No, we just want to knaa aboot proper art.

Lyon Proper art.

Harry Yes, not all this stuff about the school of the Renaissance.

Oliver We just want to be able to look at a picture and know what it means.

Lyon Ah, but what do you mean? 'What it means'?

George What do you think we mean? 'What it means'? We mean the meaning.

Lyon Exactly. But what do you mean by 'the meaning'?

George What the hell do you think we mean by 'the meaning'? That's what we hired you for. Listen, mate, if you divvint knaa the meaning of the meaning, what bloody chance have we got?

Lyon But this is the point of the lecture. What something means is not self-evident.

George What do you mean, it's not self-evident? It's a picture, isn't it? It's on the wall. It's clear as day.

Harry Look, all we want to do is to look at a picture and see what you see in it.

Lyon But what I see in it is informed by all of the other pictures I have seen. Does that mean it has no meaning for you?

George To be quite honest – no, it doesn't. We divvint want to graft all day and come up to look at pictures of cherubs and that.

Harry We want to see art that means something.

Lyon But all art means something.

Jimmy Docs it?

Oliver I think you're getting confused here – all we want to do is look at an ordinary picture of something and understand it.

Jimmy Ne fancy stuff about the meaning of meaning – just straightforward . . . art appreciation.

Lyon But this is Art Appreciation.

Harry But we want to knaa the secret behind what's gannin' on.

Lyon But there are no secrets – it's all there in front of you.

George But there must be a secret to it.

Lyon Of course there's not.

Young Lad Well, if there's not a secret – how come we divvint knaa what's gannin' on?

Lyon I think you might be looking for the wrong thing. There's no secret to art – that's the point – everything's there in front of you, there's nothing to 'understand' – the point of painting is how it makes you feel.

George Feel?

Oliver What do you mean?

Lyon What you feel – emotionally. The 'meaning' of a painting is not in the painting – it's in the observer.

Jimmy The what?

Lyon The person who's looking at the painting. Or at least in the relationship between the observer and the painting.

Jimmy Are you sure?

George Hang on. So now you're saying paintings don't have a meaning . . .

Lyon Yes and no. Of course they have a meaning – they mean something to you. You have to understand your own emotional sensibility.

Jimmy Has anybody any idea what he's talking about?

Lyon The point is not to examine a painting – but to 'feel' a painting.

Jimmy Listen, if you came here and telt wi to feel a sculpture that would be one thing. But feeling a picture – it's just ganna be flat, man.

Lyon You're looking for answers. Art isn't about answers – art is about asking questions. How do you feel about this woman? How do you feel about this colour, green?

George How do we feel about green?

Young Lad What do you mean? Green is green. You divvint feel anything about green. You look at green, it's just a colour.

Lyon The green of a summer lawn, the green of your mother's eyes?

George Now look here – we ordered you because you were supposed to be the professor of the University. Turns out you're not even at a university and your great claim to fame is you've been on holiday with someone we've never heard of. Listen, we don't want to hear about the High Renaissance or the feeling of the colour green. We just want the basic facts. We want to look at a picture – there on the wall – and knaa what it means, ne messing about with the feeling of feeling. What's so difficult about that?

Lyon Because there are no facts. Art's an art, it's not a science!

George Well, how the hell are you going to teach wi, then?

Lyon I don't know. I really don't know.

They've come to a complete impasse. Silence. They all look at Lyon – who is completely shaken.

Do it yourselves! That's it. You do it.

Oliver What do you mean, 'You do it'?

Lyon No. I'm sorry. It doesn't matter.

George No, speak yer mind, son.

Lyon Paint.

Oliver Paint?!

Lyon Draw, paint, whatever it takes, do it yourself.

George Us?

Oliver Paint paintings?

Lyon Why not?

Jimmy But they'll be rubbish.

Lyon Yes. But it doesn't matter – it's not about technical proficiency. It's about understanding 'why' an artist makes the choices he does.

George We can't do that.

Harry Praxis. Marx, isn't it? 'Hitherto, the world has been interpreted as an object of contemplation, not as sensuous human activity.' *Theses on Feuerbach*, isn't it? It's ne good just looking at the world, you have to change it. Theory in action. Practico-critical activity.

George Shut up, Harry – Look, nebody's deing any painting in this art class.

Young Lad What?

George It's categorically unconstitutional.

Harry What do you mean, it's unconstitutional?

George Article 13, Section 4 – no one shall be engaged in an activity which could be used for financial gain or practical employment.

Young Lad What's wrang with practical employment?

George Watch it, you.

Lyon It's just an exercise. Nobody's going to see it.

George Are you trying to get me barred? They'd have me up in front of the regional committee, son.

Oliver Look. Nebody cares if we paint a few pictures.

Lyon Anyway, the point is not to learn to paint – the painting is to learn about art. Let me talk to them.

George All right. But on your head be it.

Harry So what we ganna paint then?

Lyon In the first instance I don't think you should paint at all.

Harry For christsakes!

*Change of light. Noise of drilling. We cut from the scene.
Actors change places and costumes, some slides are
shown of the group at work, perhaps some other slides
indicate some prescient economic facts, till another slide
announces:*

ONE WEEK LATER

*A siren sounds and lights go up on a new scene. There
is a new image, showing the guys at work in the hut.
The third screen is blank till we need it later in the scene.*

Lyon OK. Who wants to go first?

Nobody offers.

What about you?

Young Lad I didn't de one.

George What do you mean, you didn't de one?

Young Lad I didn't know what to do.

George What do you mean, you didn't know what to
do? You were meant to do a lino cut.

Young Lad But it didn't make sense.

George What didn't make sense? A bairn can do a lino
cut.

Young Lad No. 'Work'. How am I supposed to draw
'work'?

Lyon That's the whole point of the exercise. We want to
see what 'work' means to you.

Young Lad But I divvint knaa what it means. I've never
been to work.

George Aye, and ye wanna think about that, lad.

Young Lad I do. Every day. Why do you think I've been up at five every morning standing outside of every pit in Ashington?

George Sit down.

Young Lad So get off my back, Uncle George.

Lyon OK. OK. How about somebody else? Jimmy.

Jimmy I didn't de one either.

George Ah, for Christ's sake.

Jimmy Actually I did de one, but I threw it away.

George What do you mean, you threw it away?

Jimmy It was absolute rubbish, so I hoyed it oot.

Oliver But that's the point, man, Jimmy. You have to bring in what you've done so's we can analyse it.

Lyon Has anybody managed to do one?

Oliver I had a go – but I divvint think it's any good.

Oliver gets his lino cut out. He puts it up on the easel. They stare at it.

Jimmy Did ye de that?

Oliver It was me fourth attempt, like. It was quite hard thinking about it inside out.

Harry What do you mean – inside out?

We see the image on the third screen.

Oliver You have to do everything the other way round. So you're carving out light.

George Is that his heed?

Oliver Aye.

Young Lad It's a bit small, isn't it?

George Shut it, you – you've never even done one.

Lyon I think the smallness is intentional, it emphasises the muscularity, the sheer physical nature of the work.

Oliver Actually, I couldn't de it any bigger 'cos I'd already carved the roof out.

Jimmy And what's this supposed to be?

Oliver His shoulder.

A detail of the shoulder is projected on the third screen.

Jimmy It looks like a horse's leg.

George Well, maybe he meant it to look like a horse's leg.

Jimmy Did you mean it to look like a horse's leg?

We flick through slides detailing various aspects of the etching.

Oliver No, of course I didn't mean it to look like a horse's leg. Look, this is me first go.

George Mind, I like his boots, though.

Jimmy Aye, admittedly the boots are very well done. But I've never seen anyone with a shoulder like that.

Lyon But look how well it conveys the sheer bulk, the brute force of the miner at the coal face.

Jimmy But that's what I'm saying – ye divvint send somebody big doon there with a shoulder like that on him. You send little wiry fellas. Like me.

Lyon But I don't think we should necessarily judge art on whether it's factually accurate. In art it's completely appropriate to exaggerate for emphasis. Look at how Oliver has drawn the roof so low –

Jimmy Low?

Lyon Look how he's bent over for dramatic effect.

Jimmy Low. I've been crawling round on me belly all week, man.

Lyon In the mine?

Jimmy No, on the allotment. Of course down the mine.

Lyon But isn't it terribly claustrophobic?

Oliver Wey aye, but how else are you going to get the coal out?

Harry Well – if you were nationalised there'd be investment in proper machinery. Do you think yer Soviet miners are crawling round all day on their bellies with picks in their hand? They've got the latest machinery. And the yields is better.

George What do you know about it? You're a bloody a dentist.

Harry I'm a socialist – and as far as I'm concerned this is a glorification of the exploitation of the common man. You want to be drawing something critical. Something that exposes the underlying inequities of the capitalist system.

Jimmy Anyway, he waddn't get much coal out like that, his leg'd gan to sleep, for a start.

Oliver It's meant to be a picture, not a manual of coal mining.

Jimmy I thought this was supposed to be Art Appreciation – what's wrang with saying what's wrang with it?

Young Lad What's wrang with it is the light.

George What?

On the screen we see details of the lamp, and of the shadows cast.

Young Lad The light, looka. If the lamp's ower there, all this shining here is wrang, isn't it? It wouldn't light up these bits. It would be shining here.

George What de ye knaa? Anyway he can light up what he likes, it's his painting.

Young Lad No, but that's the whole thing about lino-cutting, isn't it? Light and dark.

George Well, keep yer opinions to yerself. Ne wonder ye can't get work.

Oliver He's right, George.

Lyon I think these formal things are very important. Of course the chiaroscuro is very limited, but what is very successful is the feeling of a man at work.

The screen goes blank.

Harry I disagree – that's exactly where he's gannin' wrong.

George What do you mean?

Harry It's not 'actually' about work – is it? It's just a depiction of work.

George What would ye knaa? You've never done a day's work in yer life. Stood there mixing stuff up for people's false teeth.

Harry Can you get off my back? It wasn't my fault that I was gassed.

Lyon Please. Gentlemen.

George Come on – let's see yours, then.

Harry gets his work out.

Harry There.

Harry's picture is shown on the screen.

Jimmy Noo, that's what I call a shoulder!

George What's that chain deing?

Harry What d'ye mean?

Jimmy He'll have his arm off with them chains.

Harry's picture remains on the screen, but on the second and third screens we see the details being talked about when they are mentioned.

Oliver What are they deing attached to that wheel?

Harry They're not chains. That's the whole point, man.

George What do you mean – they're not chains?

Oliver Well, what are they?

Harry Metaphors.

Jimmy I beg yer pardon.

Harry It's not a chain. It's a metaphor. Isn't it?

Jimmy I don't follow.

Harry What it's saying is: work is the creation of surplus value expropriated by bourgeois class interests.

George And they are chains of oppression tied to the wheel of industry.

Harry It's just a wheel, actually.

Jimmy So what's that clock dein'?

Harry Tellin' the time – it's the tyranny of the wage-slave system. The tyranny of working to the clock.

Jimmy That's fantastic. How did you think of that?

Harry It's obvious, isn't it?

George So what's that pipe dein'?

Harry What do you mean – what's that pipe dein'?

George Well, if that's the wheel of industry –

Harry That's not the wheel of industry – it's just a wheel.

Young Lad Impotence.

George I beg your pardon?

They all look at him.

Young Lad It's a sign of impotence.

They are still puzzled.

George What ye on aboot?

We see a close-up of the pipe, then an even closer view of the pipe appears on the next screen.

Young Lad It's a Freudian symbol, isn't it?

Jimmy A what?

Harry No, it isn't.

Young Lad It is. I'm telling you that is a Freudian symbol.

Harry No, it isn't.

George How the hell would ye knaa?

Young Lad We did it in an Introduction to Psychology.

George Harry – is that a Freudian symbol?

Harry Of course it isn't a Freudian symbol – it's just a pipe.

Young Lad Exactly – a pipe's one of the best Freudian symbols you can get.

George It's absolutely ridiculous.

Jimmy What the hell is a Freudian symbol?

Young Lad It's aboot the things that are ganning on in yer heed that you divvint realise, and they all come oot – as a Freudian symbol.

Harry Listen, I'm the one who did this and I'm telling ye, it's got nowt to do with Freudian symbols – this is about politics and that's that.

Young Lad That's the point of Freudian symbols – you divvint even knaa yer deing them. If you tried to de a Freudian symbol then it wouldn't be a Freudian symbol at aal.

Jimmy What the hell would it be, then?

Young Lad Just a symbol.

Harry This is absolutely ridiculous.

George (*to the Young Lad*) Listen, you're only here on sufferance. So watch what you're saying.

Jimmy I still don't understand what it's supposed to be doing.

Oliver It's supposed to make you think.

Jimmy Is art supposed to make you think?

Harry Course it does. All art makes you think. Oliver's made you think – made you think what it was like to work doon a hole – but it didn't necessarily make you think about the economic conditions, did it though?

Jimmy Look – nebody wants to think about economic conditions while they're looking at a picture.

Harry What the hell's wrong with looking at economic conditions? What d'ye want to de – stick yer heed in the sand and condemn yersel to exploitation?

Jimmy Nebody wants to see people hewing coal or folks chained to cogs or any of that malarkey. I thowt this was ganna be an art class – I thowt we'd be drawing flowers or nice furry animals and that kinda thing. Not diagrams of the coal industry. Anyway I don't want to see drawings of us doon the bloody pit.

Oliver What's wrong with working down a pit like?

Jimmy Nowt – I just de it all day long.

Harry Exactly – and that is why it's every man's duty to attack the fundamental principles of capitalist production.

Jimmy In a lino cut?!

Harry Ye have to start somewhere.

Jimmy I couldn't even de a fella walking alang a road, nivver mind undermining the capitalist means of production.

George Anyway, if you want to be undermining capitalism you wanna be out there organising a union of dental workers, not deing lino cuts.

Lyon Gentlemen . . .

George Well, where were you in '26, eh?

Young Lad I don't see how this is Art Appreciation – all you ever do is slag each other off.

Harry I was convalescing after a relapse eight years on from being gassed in the Somme. Where were you in

1918 when I was in the trenches? Making a tidy sum for the Duke of Portland.

George Look. There's ne need to pull rank just 'cos yer a cripple.

Lyon Look, there's nothing wrong with politics, we're all 'fellow travellers' here. It's just art can be so much more. You're thinking about this the wrong way. We don't go to art to find out about the world, we go to art to find out about ourselves.

Jimmy Do ye?

Lyon Look. Why don't we try something completely neutral?

Young Lad Like what?

Lyon I don't know. A religious theme, perhaps?

Harry Oh for christsakes!

The siren sounds.
   Blackout.

The sound of rain. The slide projector clicks on:

'THE DELUGE' BY OLIVER KILBOURN

And on the other slide projector: image of 'The Deluge'.
   Oliver talks over the image.

Oliver I started after the foreshift. I took the paints and that, but I had no idea what I was supposed to be doing. I just looked at this blank bit of card. I didn't knaa what a deluge was supposed to look like. I mean, I've seen a storm – but a deluge. And I was completely stuck, you know. So I just started painting these lines. I wasn't thinking – I was just painting. Throwing on lines just to de something – and then it all clicked, and it just came

27

pouring out – all this feeling – the little houses being swept away, the teeming water – it all just came out. And when I stopped to look at what I'd done, suddenly I realised it was light – it was morning – time for work – I thought it'd been an hour or something – I'd been on the whole night. And I was shaking – literally shaking – 'cos for the first time in me life, I'd really achieved something – I had made something that was mine – not for someone else – not for money – not for anything really. And I felt like for those few hours there – I was me own boss.

Jimmy That's incredible, Oliver.

Oliver It's weird, I never thought I could do anything like that.

Lyon I think it's a remarkable piece of work. Jolly well done.

Oliver sits down.

Now, anyone else?

Jimmy gets up and sets his picture up.
    The click of the slide projector. White light – then click a picture of a Bedlington terrier.

George It's of a dog.

Jimmy I knaa it's of a dog.

George But it was meant to be aboot a deluge.

Jimmy I knaa – I started deein a deluge but it turned into a dog.

Oliver A whippet!

Jimmy No – it's a Bedlington terrier.

George It's ne good doing a class if your not ganna stick to the exercises . . .

Young Lad I think it's quite good, actually.

George It doesn't matter if it's good or not – it's not a blooming deluge.

Jimmy I thought yous weren't ganna be judgemental.

Harry Of course we're ganna be judgemental – it's an Art Appreciation class.

Lyon The most important thing is to take the picture on its own merits. I want everyone to look at the painting, and discuss what James has done – what it is rather than what it isn't.

They don't really get this instruction, but they do as they're told. They look at the picture. Finally . . .

George That bloke's a bit small.

Oliver Presumably that's just the perspective.

Jimmy No – I just didn't think I'd be to fit a big one in. I started the dog a bit big, see.

George But look at the size of that wheelbarrow – it's as big as a wagon. And what's them pots deing in the middle of the field?

Jimmy I divvint knaa – I just felt like drawing them.

Lyon I think the point about this picture is that things don't have to be realistically depicted to have an expressive effect.

Harry Why did you paint the kennel the same colour as the grass?

Jimmy I'd run oot've broon by that point. Anyway the kennel was more of an afterthought. I telt yees ye waddn't like it.

Lyon On the contrary, I think it's a wonderful piece of untutored art.

Jimmy Well, if I'm untutored weys fault's that like?

Oliver It was meant to be a compliment, man.

George I still divvint knaa what it's got to do with a deluge.

Harry That's the whole point of the exercise. It doesn't matter what it is – what matters is what it means.

George OK, so what does it mean?

Jimmy It doesn't mean anything – it's just a Bedlington errier.

George See. It's not about meaning, is it? It's about trying to express werselves.

Jimmy Exactly, and I expressed myself about a Bedlington terrier.

Lyon The point is that James has painted something that has a direct connection to him. Yes, this fellow here is a little small and the kennel could possibly have benefited from another colour. But it's immediate. Full of a feeling for its material.

Harry I divvint see that there's any feeling at all. It's just a meaningless scene.

Lyon But the feeling is in the clear-sightedness. The lack of pretension. James set out to paint a whippet –

Jimmy A Bedlington terrier.

Lyon And he did so simply – without much technique, but with a great clarity of purpose, and as a painting, it is that which recommends itself to us.

George But it was supposed to be a deluge.

Harry But even so – the whole idea of the exercise was to interpret something, wasn't it? You gave a title and we had to interpret it. OK, it's not a deluge, but this isn't interpreting anything. It's got ne message.

Jimmy Why does it have to have a message?

Harry Why bother painting something if it doesn't have a message?

Lyon Because it might be beautiful, for instance.

Harry A whippet!?

Jimmy You're doing this deliberately.

Young Lad Well, maybe it has a message. Maybe it tells people about Ashington who've never been here.

Harry Aye, but who the hell's gonna see it? Us. I divvint need to know about bloody whippets. Art has to say something, less it's just . . .

George What?

Harry Decoration. I'm sick of all these exercises. You've telt wi – to draw what we know – cut out all the politics, to me I can't see what the point is. 'The Deluge'. It's all very well, but I want to do something with a proper meaning – something relevant to our lives.

Lyon Should we move on to yours, in that case?

Harry No. It's rubbish.

Jimmy Well, according to you, so was mine.

Harry It's exactly the same problem. It doesn't really mean owt.

He gets it out and puts it on an easel. It is 'The East Wind'. As it is put up a projection shows a larger version.

Young Lad The deluge?

31

Harry Well, I wanted to do something more from round here. I'm not interested in biblical storms.

George It's good this, man.

Oliver It's brilliant, Harry.

Jimmy What do you mean, 'It's rubbish'?

Harry Like I said. OK, it's a bit better than your whippet. But it's just a scene.

Lyon It's actually a really excellent exercise in two-point perspective.

Harry Exactly. Oh yes – everything looks right. Lovely buildings the right colour, and all the folk are the right size. But it says nowt.

Oliver What are you on about, Harry?

George Admittedly it's raining, but is it technically a deluge though?

Harry Exactly – there is no deluge, is there? That's the point. You didn't want me to draw ideas, you specifically asked for something neutral. Well, there it is. 'Cos that's what happens round here. Nowt. No deluges, no big ideas. Nowt.

Oliver But don't you see it is political, Harry?

Harry Political. If it was political it would have the open sewers down the middle of the street, like just around the corner. If I wanted to be political I'd've drawn the fella next door dying of emphysema.

Oliver I think you're missing the point. No. It's not about how you've drawn it. It's about what you've drawn, Harry.

Harry What have I drawn?

Oliver Us.

Harry What do you mean?

Oliver You've drawn us. In the street – it's us, Harry. We've all been in that wind.

Jimmy We've all been in that shop.

George Shut up, man, Jimmy.

Harry And what's political about that?

Oliver Because it shows who we are. Don't you see? It works on loads of levels. OK, first it's a picture of a street corner, but then it's a story, isn't it – about some folk who are heading into the wind and the others who are waiting round the corner. One side you'll get blown over – one side yer alreet. It's like a metaphor, but it's not just a metaphor, 'cos it is what it is. It's just a picture of a street.

Jimmy And how is that political, again?

Oliver It's a parable – about facing a storm.

Jimmy Is that reet, Harry? Is that what you meant?

Oliver It doesn't matter what Harry meant. It's what's there.

George Aye, but you have to ask what it's supposed to mean.

Lyon But that's what I've been trying to say. Maybe, in art, Harry needn't know the meaning. Maybe the meaning is not with Harry.

Young Lad It's with the art.

Oliver It's with whoever's looking at it.

George So you can just make up anything you want it to mean?

33

Lyon No, the meaning is in the interaction of all these things. Art is a place where all of these conflicts are resolved. Isn't that the point of art? We're trying to resolve things. Make something beautiful.

Young Lad Like a higher force.

Jimmy What, like God?

Lyon Spirituality. For want of a better word. Yes, like God.

Harry Listen, Mr Lyon. I've been in the Somme. I've seen lads blown to little bits. There is no God, Mr Lyon. There is no higher power ganna sort things out or make things mean anything. Beauty – you've got to be joking. There's nothing beautiful about living round here.

Siren. Freeze. Lighting change. Exit Harry, Jimmy, George, Young Lad. Just Lyon and Oliver are left.
    There is now a projection of Lyon painting his mural. On the other screen we see the half-finished painting.
    Lyon dons his smock and stands, palette in hand, before his painting. Title:

OLIVER BORROWS SOME BOOKS

Oliver Hello

Lyon Hello, Oliver.

Oliver Hello, Mr Lyon. I'm sorry to disturb you.

Lyon Not at all, please come in.

Oliver Wow. Did you paint this?

Lyon Yes. It's a sketch for a mural I'm painting for Essex County Council.

Oliver It's amazing. I didn't think you'd be here on a Saturday. I came down on the train to gan to the library to look up some of them things you mentioned. And I thowt I'd take a look in since I was here.

Lyon Well, I'm very glad you did.

Oliver It's a pity you can't borrow books if yer from out of Newcastle. I can't get over this. You must think we're a right bunch of amateurs.

Lyon On the contrary, I've been incredibly moved by what the group has done.

Oliver I know, but when you see this stuff – well, it's in a different league, isn't it?

Lyon This is done in a very different context. I think what has amazed me is the connection to what you paint. It's very unusual.

Oliver I knaa, but we can't paint properly. Like you can.

Lyon What you are seeing is technique, you mustn't confuse this with the quality of expression. Good art simply radiates – it should bring light in, it should order experience, all of those civilising things. Anybody can learn draughtsmanship.

Oliver I divvint knaa – I'd never be to do that.

Lyon Yes, you could.

Oliver Me?

Lyon From what I've seen – it'd take two years at the most with the basic teaching.

Oliver So you could actually teach me?

Lyon No. What you're doing is much more important than learning technique. What you are doing: your sense of discovery, the way you are integrating the study of art

35

with your life, your creativity. Don't you see how exciting this is? That's how art should be taught, that's what art should be. I really didn't think this would work, but don't you see what you've achieved? Look at how you've painted working down the pit, look at how sophisticated it's become. Each painting is such a huge leap forward.

Oliver You really think so?

Lyon Yes, I do.

Oliver You know, Mr Lyon, when I started this, something just clicked – I just felt like I'd found something simple, ye knaa, something I could do, something I was really good at. And every week I come into the class and I look at what Harry's done, and he's streets ahead, every time, and I'm not so sure any more.

Lyon This isn't a race, Oliver.

Oliver Can I ask you a straightforward question – am I any good?

Lyon It's not a question of good and bad – that's what I'm trying to teach you.

Oliver I know, but I don't want to waste my time on something if I'm not good at it.

Lyon I think you have a real feel for this. You are as talented as anyone who comes through here. But more than that you are serious about it. Art isn't about painting a picture. Art is a journey. And it can last a whole life. A place where you understand your whole life from.

Oliver You really think I could do it?

Lyon Look here – take these. (*Giving books.*)

Oliver Roger Fry.

Lyon And this. This is very good. Ruskin.

Oliver Are you sure?

Lyon Of course I'm sure. This is the essential work of any artist. Cultivating a sensibility.

Oliver And it tells you that in here?

Lyon No, the hard bit is you have to work that out for yourself. Art's about you. About knowing thyself. But Roger Fry is very interesting about Cézanne.

Oliver Thank you, Mr Lyon. I can't thank you enough.

Lyon It's a very great pleasure, Oliver.

Change of scene again. Crashing noises. Film of the coal face: as before, it's harsh and the whole feel of all this cuts across the naturalism of the scene.

George, Oliver, Harry, Young Lad and Jimmy all come on and prepare the stage for the next scene. This is clearly not done in character but we get the feel of what the start of a class might have been like.

When the stage is set the lights change and the guys snap into character. A young woman of about twenty immediately appears at the 'door' of the class. Project:

THE VISIT

Susan Hello.

They all stare at her as if they've seen a ghost.

Young Lad Hello?

George What are you doing?

Susan I've come for the art class.

George You can't come in here, pet.

Susan But this is the art class, isn't it?

Young Lad Yes.

George No. I mean . . .

Harry I don't think you understand, pet. This is an art class – for men.

Susan Yes, I know all about it. Where do you want me to take them off?

George I beg yer pardon.

Susan Normally, there's a side room – but really I'm not that fussy.

George I don't understand. Take what off?

Susan Me clothes. If it's a problem I could just as easy to do it in the corner.

Oliver Am I hearing right?

George Just wait a minute. You'll stay right there, young lady – fully clothed.

Jimmy I think I better sit doon.

George Have you lost yer senses? Coming in here threatening to expose yourself to all and sundry. What you thinking of? This is the WEA, for God's sake.

Susan I've come all the way from Newcastle.

George (*to the Young Lad*) I've never heard anything like this in my life.

    Lyon comes in in a rush of energy.

Lyon Look, I'm terribly sorry. The train again. Let's not waste any time. Jimmy, get the easels out – ah, Susan, pop yourself in the cupboard there and we can get started.

George Hang on a minute!

Lyon Oliver, put yours up over there, and –

George You know each other?

Lyon Well, of course. Susan – let's get down to business.

George Wait a minute. She can't go in there.

Lyon Why not?

George The Scouts go in there.

Susan It's all right. Just tell them to knock.

George I don't know what you're playing at, young lady, but you are not taking your clothes off here, there or anywhere else for that matter.

Jimmy Hang on – let's not be too hasty.

George Shut it, you.

Young Lad I divvint see what's wrang with it – she's not deing any harm.

George You an' all. This is an executive matter and there'll be no nudity in here . . .

Susan Will somebody tell me what's going on here?

George We might ask you the same thing, pet.

Lyon Susan is going to pose for us. I thought it would be a special treat.

George A treat. You'll bring us into disrepute.

Lyon I'm very sorry. I should have explained this all before. I just thought it might be something to liven things up.

Harry Liven things up! If wor lass finds oot it'll be the end of Monday neets aal together.

Oliver Look – it's alreet, pet. Why divvint you sit ower there with yer clays on. We don't want to embarrass you or anything.

Susan Oh, I really don't mind.

Jimmy Neither do I.

George Watch it, or I'll have ye barred.

Oliver You're not really expecting us to just sit here with somebody stark naked?

Lyon It's completely normal practice.

Oliver It might be where you come from, but I've never seen a woman naked.

Young Lad Neither have I.

George If you'd had the misfortune to see wor lass you'd not be so keen right now. This has got nothing to do with who has seen what. There is no way I am allowing a young woman to run around here completely naked – full stop.

Susan Oh, I'm not completely naked – usually I'm covered with a drape.

Harry Anyway, I'm not being a part of asking a young girl like that to take her clothes off – it's out-and-out exploitation.

Susan It's quite good money, actually.

Lyon How can you understand the human form if you don't draw from life? There's nothing lewd about this. Life drawing has been an essential part of art training since the Ancient Greeks.

George Greeks! It might be all right for you in Jesmond – swanning around with divorcees. But we've got proper standards here, lad.

The girl has given her coat to the Young Lad and is starting to unbutton her blouse. George grabs her and pushes her coat into her hand.

Put yer coat on, young lady. Does your mother know about this?

Susan My mother's dead. Anyway, there's absolutely nothing wrong with it. I do it twice a week at the University.

Lyon Look, can we please get started? It's nearly half past.

Harry You should get yourself a proper job, young lady, instead of parading your arse around to all and sundry.

Susan I've got a proper job at Carricks, actually – I just do this for some extra money.

George Well, you should be ashamed of yourself.

Lyon Please –

Susan I'm not ashamed of anything. I'm paying myself through art school. Besides there's nothing wrong with the female form.

Young Lad I agree, actually . . .

A noise outside.

Oliver What's that?

Lyon Oh God.

Harry goes to the window.

Harry What the hell's that?

Lyon Look, everybody. Please get your work out. To the easels.

George Bloody hell.

They crowd round the window but Oliver can't see.

Oliver What is it?

Jimmy It's a Rolls-Roycc!

Oliver With a chauffeur!

Lyon Look – there's no need to be alarmed.

Young Lad There's a wife getting out.

Jimmy With a hat.

Lyon Please – will everybody sit down.

Susan Do you want me to take me clothes off or what?

Lyon Will everybody just SIT DOWN!

Helen Sutherland enters, they are agog.

Helen!

Helen Sutherland Robert, darling. Sorry I'm late.

Jimmy Jesus Christ – she's not ganna get her kit off inall?

Helen Sutherland All these little streets look the same.

George I'm sorry, Madam, who might I be talking to?

Helen Sutherland Helen Sutherland. How do you do?

Lyon Miss Sutherland – is a collector of art.

Helen Sutherland Oh, I don't know about that. I have one or two paintings. I'm not really a collector – more of an enthusiast, really.

Lyon Miss Sutherland has several Nicholsons and a Mondrian.

Susan A Mondrian!

Jimmy A what?

Susan Piet Mondrian. He's a Dutch painter – mostly does squares.

Helen Sutherland Rectangles, actually.

Lyon Miss Sutherland is particularly interested in modern art.

Jimmy Well, you've come to right place, pet. Most of these were done this week.

Helen Sutherland Ah, delightful.

Lyon Miss Sutherland is the heiress to the P&O Line.

Helen Sutherland Please, no one is interested in me.

George Hang on a minute. Nebody said anything to me about a visiting heiress. This should have gone through the proper channels.

Lyon I'm really sorry. We met at supper on Saturday and I took the liberty of inviting her up here – if the train wasn't so late, I would have had the chance to explain . . .

Helen sees George's painting.

Helen Sutherland Well, this is awfully sweet. You've painted all of these yourselves. Ah – look at this – very interesting indeed.

George That's mine, actually.

Helen Sutherland Yes, very interesting – a lovely sense of line.

43

George Thank you very much.

Helen Sutherland What is it?

George Well – it's a miner, Ma'am.

Helen Sutherland I can see it's a miner – I mean what were you using?

George Oh, just a bit of emulsion and an old board I found in the yard.

Helen Sutherland And you did this from imagination?

George Well – from memory, like.

Helen Sutherland So you've actually been underground?

George Wey, yes. I'm a miner.

Helen Sutherland Goodness – how awful.

Jimmy We're all miners, actually – apart from Harry, who got gassed in the war. And the young lad, but he doesn't count.

Young Lad I really only come 'cos it's warm.

Lyon The class is part of the WEA. It's an open intake – everybody here is entirely non-professional.

Helen Sutherland Are you a miner too, dear?

Susan No – I only came up to take me clothes off, but I don't know why I bothered.

Helen Sutherland Please – don't mind me. What is this, exactly?

George That's a pit prop, Miss. You put the props up to keep the ceiling up when you dig out a seam. It's actually much more of a difficult job than you might imagine.

Helen Sutherland (*uninterested in George's description*) It must be terribly dreary. I do like how grey it is. I'm terribly fond of grey. Well, jolly well done. A wonderful sense of form. Very intuitive.

She moves on.

And what's this?

Oliver That's mine. I haven't unwrapped it.

Lyon This is Oliver Kilbourn, one of the more promising students.

Helen Sutherland Would you mind if I saw it?

Oliver Not really, like.

Oliver unwraps it.

Young Lad That's amazing!

George Bloody hell, Oliver.

Jimmy Look, that's George Elliot.

George It's incredible.

Jimmy Did you really just do that?

Lyon This really is a huge leap forward, Oliver.

Oliver I've been looking at a lot of Sickert. I went down to the Library in Newcastle. I'm interested in the sense of a community. You know, like his ones of the music hall.

Helen Sutherland Where is this exactly?

Oliver It's the club.

Helen Sutherland The club?

Oliver Yes.

Helen Sutherland Is it somewhere you actually go?

Oliver Well, I'm not really much of a clubman meself. But we've all been at one time.

Helen Sutherland I see.

Oliver To be quite honest with you, I just work and paint really.

Helen Sutherland Sounds jolly sensible to me. It looks terribly crowded.

Oliver Well, it's a Saturday.

Helen Sutherland He's making some kind of public address, I take it.

Oliver He's probably singing some darkie songs or what not.

Helen Sutherland There don't seem to be many women there.

Oliver Well, no – it's the club. Women are barred, aren't they?

Helen Sutherland (*patronisingly*) I suspect they're rather grateful. Absolutely terrific – very well done. Now what have we her? Mmm – interesting – very interesting.

She looks at Jimmy's picture of flowers.

Jimmy Well, I knaa it's not much good – but I like to have a go.

Helen Sutherland Really very interesting. And where is this exactly?

Jimmy That's wor hoose.

Helen Sutherland And these are peonies?

Jimmy No, they're flowers actually. I've done a couple of ponies before but I couldn't get their heeds right. This is a table with flowers on.

Helen Sutherland And what's this here?

Jimmy Oh, that's an afterthought. It seemed a bit boring just having a wall – so I put that in. It's what I keep me comb in – and that's a mirror. Or at least a bit of a mirror. I only did part – 'cos I couldn't get the rest in.

Helen Sutherland And this is a vase, I take it?

Jimmy Aye – we inherited it from the wife's mother.

Helen Sutherland Interesting change of colour towards the edge here.

Jimmy That was a mistake – but there's a canny bit of perspective on that table, tho'.

Helen Sutherland I very much like the yellow.

Jimmy It's not really yellow. It's green in real life, but I had a big tin of yellow left ower from the shed.

Helen Sutherland Well, I like it. And the grey – a very nice grey.

Jimmy Oh aye – a very canny colour, grey. That's a net curtain.

Helen Sutherland Oh, really?

Jimmy Oh, I knaa – it came oot a right dog's dinner, so I coloured it in. We've not really learnt how to do see-through.

Lyon It's not essentially a class about technique.

Jimmy I only really come here to get oot of hoose.

Helen Sutherland I'd like to buy it.

Jimmy What?!

Helen Sutherland I'd like to buy it.

Jimmy Yer joking, aren't you?

Helen Sutherland Most certainly not. Would two pounds be enough?

Jimmy Two pound! I can't charge two pound for this.

Helen Sutherland I'd really not like to spend much more. Three is my final offer.

Harry Three quid for that!

Young Lad You're not actually ganna buy it, are you?

Lyon Are you sure you wouldn't like to see some more?

Jimmy Listen – I divvint want yer money, man, you can have it for nowt.

George Hang on a minute.

Jimmy What's the matter now?

George You absolutely cannot do that.

Jimmy I can't charge three quid for it.

George It's not yours to give away.

Jimmy What do ya mean, it's not mine?

George It belangs to the WEA.

Jimmy That's absolutely ridiculous. I paid for that paint mesel'. That's high gloss, that is.

George But the copyright belangs to the WEA.

Jimmy Copyright?!

Harry He's right. You couldn't've painted that without the auspices of the group.

Jimmy Yes, I could.

George No you couldn't.

Harry You couldn't've painted that without Mr Lyon's instruction.

Jimmy What ye on aboot? I've never done one of his exercises yet.

George That's not the point.

Jimmy What do you mean, that's not the point?

George I think we'll have to refer this to the regional committee.

Jimmy This is absolutely ridiculous. That's my painting and I'll de what I want with it.

Harry No it's not – the whole principle of the WEA is about collective ownership.

Jimmy Look – if she wants the thing, I don't see why she shouldn't have it.

Lyon Are you sure you don't want some of the other ones?

Helen Sutherland No – this is the one I like. I think all of the stuff underground's rather dreary. I think this has a certain spiritual quality.

George Well, I'm afraid you can't have it. It's confiscated.

Jimmy Hang on a minute.

George I'm overruling you.

Susan I don't see why she should't have it.

George Shut up, you.

Susan I didn't come here to be spoken to like that.

Susan goes off in a huff.

Jimmy If we're not allowed to sell it, why can't we just give it to her?

George That's not the point.

Young Lad If it's for free, it's not for profit, is it?

George But it's the property of the group.

Jimmy But we haven't even got anywhere to keep it. Have you been in that storeroom?

George Well, put them up at home.

Jimmy You've got to be joking – the wife waddnt give it wall space. Look, pet, ye can have it gratis and there's a few in the back I'll throw in an' all.

George Is anyone listening to me? That painting's going nowhere.

Helen Sutherland Look – I don't want to cause problems.

Harry Anyway, we shouldn't be giving owt away. This is a record of our history. We should be keeping it all together.

Jimmy History. What a load of old rubbish – it's a painting of a table. I don't mind if she wants it.

Lyon Perhaps you could give a contribution to the group?

Jimmy Hang on – it's my painting.

Oliver George is reet. It's not about individuals, it's a collective effort. I've learned as much off Harry as I have off Mr Lyon.

Jimmy I haven't learnt nowt off any of yis. I can barely understand what yers are on aboot.

Helen Sutherland What did he say? Look, I'll give three pounds to the group and I'll buy you all fresh paints.

Lyon That is very generous indeed, Miss Sutherland.

Jimmy Alreet – take the short off me back. Fifty year, and this is forst thing of mine anybody's wanted. Yis can have the three quid for all I care.

George Look – nobody is taking that painting anywhere.

Young Lad This is absolutely ridiculous. Three quid for that. This isn't art. It's rubbish. All this rubbish with whippets and flowers, and pitmen at bait time. It's rubbish, man. Listen to yerselves, gannin' on every week with yer cushy little jobs. This isn't art. A proper artist would be tearing the bloomin' thing up. Political? Do yous look about? Do yous knaa what's happenin'? It's sentimental rubbish.

George You're barred.

Young Lad Well, perhaps we should put it to a vote.

George Listen, this is a democratic organisation. Nebody is voting on anything in here – there are proper procedures to go through.

Jimmy Absolute rubbish. All those in favour.

The Young Lad, Lyon, Jimmy and Oliver put their hands up.

Carried.

Helen Sutherland Marvellous. I'll have Mills drop round a cheque.

George This is absolutely unconstitutional.

Suddenly Susan appears naked, carrying a drape.

Susan And I'll have me two-and-six, inall.

The guys look at her.
Siren. Change of scene.

Furniture rearranged.
  Projection:

*Another shows the outside of Helen Sutherland's mansion,
another the view from her window. The wooden chairs
are put together to form a 'settee'.*

Jimmy Bloody hell.

Young Lad I've never seen anything like it.

  Harry goes to sit down.

I cannit believe this. Have you seen how many settees
she's got?

George Hey, man. You can't sit down.

Harry That bloke said go in and make yerself at home.

George I should have barred you when I had the chance.
You can't just sit there. They'll think yer common.

Harry We are common. You divvint think we'd be invited
up in the afternoon if we were posh? She's keeping us
away from the rest of them.

George Miss Sutherland's very kindly invited us up to
see her art. Don't be ungrateful.

Harry Don't forget, every single thing in this room's
been paid for by some poor stevedore breaking his back
in some P&O engine room sixteen hour a day.

Jimmy Yer only jealous. It's my work up there. Miss
Sutherland is a woman of taste and discernment.

Harry Rubbish – look at what it's next to.

  Jimmy reads the rubric.

'Alfred Wallis'. What a load of rubbish.

George Have you seen the clip of this one?

They all turn and look. The slide changes to show Henry Moore's sketch of 'A Woman Reclining', 1933.

Harry Look at the state of it.

George It's not even finished.

Young Lad Ne wonder she thinks Jimmy's a genius, if this is what she normally buys.

George Look at the heed on it. I thought I was bad.

Harry It wants hoying oot if you ask me.

Enter Helen Sutherland with Lyon.

Helen Sutherland I see you're admiring my Henry Moore.

Lyon Quite recent, isn't it?

Helen Sutherland '33. Exquisite, isn't it?

They all look at it again, carefully.

George To be quite honest with you, wouldn't you say the head is a bit small?

Helen Sutherland Absolutely, I love the way he emphasises the body.

Jimmy You mean that's how he meant to de it?

Helen Sutherland Of course. I think there's nobody really tackling form in the same way. I think he's perhaps our only really world-class artist.

George Who, him?

Helen Sutherland Yes. I thought you'd find an affinity with him being the son of a miner.

Jimmy A miner!

Oliver This was done by a miner?

Helen Sutherland Not exactly. He managed to get out. He went to the local academy.

Lyon And then the Royal College, of course.

Helen Sutherland I think it's why he comes to art with a very different perspective to everyone else.

Jimmy But it hasn't even got a face.

Oliver But that's the point. It's not meant to be a particular person, Jimmy. It's meant to represent the general idea.

Helen Sutherland Surely you can feel the sense of mass – the weight of the body? I always feel the intense longing when I look at it – the head remote from the cumbersome limbs, the sleek line as if carved from a sinuous block of stone, its Rembrandt-like combination of austere sadness with a real feel for physicality.

Jimmy Aye, but you have to admit he's not very good at hips.

Helen Sutherland Speaking as a woman of a certain age – I think he has a very good grasp of hips.

Oliver What do you think, Mr Lyon?

Lyon It's obviously very impressive, but I actually prefer his earlier work. I find the move towards abstraction a bit of dead end.

Helen Sutherland That's because you are a middlebrow provincial realist.

Lyon Now, now, Helen. There is nothing wrong with figurative work.

Helen Sutherland Well, what do you think of the Nicholson? I've only just bought it.

The Nicholson is completely white: a circle with a square cut out. They look at it for some time.

Jimmy Well – it's very . . . white.

Helen Sutherland It's entirely white.

Jimmy What's it supposed to be?

Helen Sutherland It's a circle on a square.

They contemplate it further.

Jimmy How much did you pay for it?

Helen Sutherland Two hundred pounds.

They contemplate it in silence.
    As the scene continues the lighting gradually drops, apart from the slide of the Nicholson, which appears more and more luminous, and the faces of the actors looking intently out front as if they are before the painting.

Jimmy I know I'm a bit stupid and everything, but I don't think I really understand what it means.

Helen Sutherland I don't think it 'means' anything specific in the traditional sense. It just is what it is – a painting.

Jimmy But I thought everything had to mean something.

Helen Sutherland It means here you all are, looking at a formal arrangement someone's made. That is what it means.

Jimmy Eh?

Oliver She means the meaning is internal to the person looking at it. The meaning is not in the objective world. The meaning is an internal thing.

Helen Sutherland Exactly. The meaning is something that happens – in your heart, in your mind – not in the world.

Young Lad But there isn't really anything there.

Helen Sutherland Precisely. We are asked not to contemplate what is, but what is not.

Young Lad But that's what I mean – what?

Helen Sutherland The numinous. The spiritual. The realm which is precisely that which we are not. The thing that binds us all together. Isn't that ultimately what we ask art to provide?

George What?

Helen Sutherland A sense of awe. Of religious awe. Of the mystery of being alive.

Young Lad What – sticking a circle on a square?

George It's a rectangle, actually. But anybody could do that. I could've done that.

Helen Sutherland But you didn't. Ben Nicholson did.

Oliver Anyway – it's not stuck on. Look.

Jimmy He's right – it's carved out.

George Aye. Look, yer right – it's all one block.

Jimmy Who'd've thought he'd gan to all that bother?

Oliver I bet it took some deing getting that circle out like that. It's a solid piece of mahogany.

They are all examining it closely.

Helen Sutherland Exactly – it's the sheer purity of the piece that really sings out. The glimpse of something beyond, something other.

Oliver I disagree. This is not about something 'beyond' anything. The whole point is – it's imperfect, isn't it? You can never have a 'perfect' circle 'cos it has to be made of something. It has to be made. That's the point. I know they call it abstract art, but it's the opposite, isn't it? It's not abstract, it's there . . . it's 'concrete'.

Jimmy Concrete?

Oliver An actual thing. And that's the beauty of it. The tension between the abstract and the concrete. It's sort of art of what it is to make art, that's what's significant.

Jimmy You've lost me.

Harry What's significant about circles and squares and a piece of wood!?

Oliver It's like a metaphor, isn't it, about taking real things and imposing shapes on them. When you know it's wood, when you feel its weight – that these geometrical shapes have been cut out of it – it means something, doesn't it? There's an effort gone in there. Work.

George Aye, so what does it mean?

Oliver It means there's a piece of wood with a square and a circle cut out. That's all.

Jimmy Well, that's profound.

Oliver It's no different from what we do really – we just make shapes on material, don't we?

George Aye, but we try to draw something.

Oliver Well, he's drawn something – carved something at least. A square and a circle. See.

Harry But a square and a circle's not in the real world.

Oliver Yes, it is.

Harry No, it isn't.

Oliver There it is! There's a square and a circle.

George Ah, but it's not real life, is it?

Oliver I don't know what's not real about that piece of wood. There it is.

George What, so you're saying art is not the real world? Art is art?

Harry You really like this, don't you? You see something in it.

Oliver Yes. I do. What I'm saying is that art is making things possible that weren't there before. Don't you see? When you're painting a painting – you're painting a painting, not painting life.

George Aye, I see what you mean.

Oliver And that is here. That thought is sort of pared down. Of course it's lots of other things. It's a landscape, it's playing with lots of different notions. But just the sheer fact of it. I think it's quite beautiful.

Lyon It's rather lost on me, I'm afraid.

Jimmy has been staring at the painting for some time and suddenly speaks as if in a reverie.

Jimmy Ye knaa – I started doon the pit when I was ten. Me mam used to get uz up at five every morning and I walked six mile ower the wagonway to Woodhorn with our kid and I went down and I was terrified. I was absolutely terrified – the dark – the noises. I hated the dark. And all the fellas – big fellas – all crushed into the cage. And they put me onto the doors – to open the doors to stop the air blaain' the wrong way. If they didn't have the doors, the air'd gan roon the quickest way and we'd all be deed. So I'd sit there all day opening the door, shutting the door – in the dark, by mesel'. I was scared stiff I was – then I went hyem and went to sleep and when the other bairns come for iz, me mam'd gan oot and tell them to gan away – and five the next morning I'm up again. Open the doors – shut the doors. They kept iz deing that for four year before they had iz on ponies. I've not had one day off – not missed a single day since 1897. Not a single day.

George What's that got to de with the painting?

The lighting snaps back into its original 'Rock Hall' state. The slides are all now views from the window.

Jimmy I divint knaa.

Helen Sutherland But what do you think of the work?

Jimmy pauses.

Jimmy Did you really pay two hundred quid for it?

Change of lighting state. Everything is taken off.

Projection:

GARDENS: ROCK HALL

A picture of the gardens. David Jones' sketch of the chapel.
On their own, Helen and Oliver.

Oliver It's lovely up here.

Helen Sutherland Yes, it's a kind of spiritual sanctuary. I don't know anywhere quite like it. I suppose it goes right back to Aidan and Cuthbert. David's painted the garden five or six times now, each time he sees something different.

59

Oliver David?

Helen Sutherland Jones. He's a poet and painter. Comes up several times a year. He never got over the trenches. I think he finds it very therapeutic.

Oliver He just comes and paints.

Helen Sutherland For a few weeks at a time.

Oliver Really. It must be lovely just to do nothing else.

Helen Sutherland Please, come.

Oliver What, me?

Helen Sutherland Yes.

Oliver Really? You wouldn't mind.

Helen Sutherland Course I wouldn't. It would be my pleasure. There is nothing I enjoy more than encouraging artists. Which is why I talked to Janet about getting an article in *The Listener* about you.

Oliver I know, but I'm not a real artist.

Helen Sutherland Of course you're a real artist.

Oliver No, I mean a real artist – that gets paid.

Helen Sutherland I don't think one can judge real art by it's monetary value. Do you?

Oliver Well, no, of course not. But it makes a difference. I mean, look at how much you spent on that painting.

Helen Sutherland That's the price, Mr Kilbourn – it has nothing to do with the value. Have you always painted?

Oliver No. It's only recent. I started down the pit when I was ten. You were supposed to be twelve officially but they turned a blind eye, 'cos me dad'd broke his back when a seam fell in and we needed the money.

Helen Sutherland I am sorry.

Oliver Me mam didn't cope very well. Went off to live in France when I was fourteen, so I had to bring up everybody by meself.

Helen Sutherland Everybody?

Oliver Well, me sister. And the bairns.

Helen Sutherland Her children?

Oliver Her fella got killed inall. I know it sounds like a bit of a sob story. But it's true – we de alreet. It's just I never had much time for meself.

Helen Sutherland You never married?

Oliver Me? No. I never really had the time. So what does Mr Sutherland think of all this art.

Helen Sutherland Mr Sutherland left us some time ago.

Oliver Oh, I'm sorry, Miss.

Helen Sutherland Don't be – it was the best thing that ever happened to me. We were married five years but it was never something Mr Sutherland physically committed himself to. He left to pursue the life of a gentleman leaving me free to pursue the arts.

Oliver Oh.

Helen Sutherland From a distance we all look like stereotypes. But look a little closer and none of our stories are typical. There's always some twist.

Oliver I don't know, I think I'm just an ordinary pitman.

Helen Sutherland I don't think you are ordinary at all.

Oliver Of course I am.

Helen Sutherland Ordinary pitmen do not paint pictures.

Oliver Yes, they do – well, we all do.

Helen Sutherland But you don't just paint pictures, Oliver, you see something different. You are sensitive to what makes art, art.

Oliver Am I?

Helen Sutherland Yes. You have an understanding. You have a gift.

Oliver So you think I could be an artist.

Helen Sutherland I think you think like an artist.

Oliver But do you think I'm any good?

Helen Sutherland What do you think?

Oliver I don't know.

Helen Sutherland Look, I'll be frank. I don't much care for all of these pictures of miners you all seem so insistent on drawing. So I can't really tell if you are a real artist or not, but I can tell you, Oliver, you have an artist's soul. Which is rare enough in itself. Whether you are good or not depends largely on how much real work you want to put in.

Oliver Oh I don't mind work, Miss.

Helen Sutherland So what if I was to give you a stipend?

Oliver A what?

Helen Sutherland A stipend. A weekly stipend. To paint.

Oliver I don't know what you mean.

Helen Sutherland A wage. A weekly wage. How much do you earn? Three, four pounds a week?

Oliver Two pound three shillings.

Helen Sutherland OK. What if I gave you two pounds, ten shillings?

Oliver To paint? And you could keep the pictures?

Helen Sutherland No, I don't want the pictures. You keep the pictures. Look at it as a gift.

Oliver I couldn't do that.

Helen Sutherland Why not?

Oliver That's your money.

Helen Sutherland Somebody gave it to me.

Oliver But I'd have to give up me job.

Helen Sutherland I don't wish to be impertinent, but isn't that the point?

Oliver But why?

Helen Sutherland Because I like you, Oliver.

Oliver You like me?

Helen Sutherland I see something of myself in you.

Oliver Me?!

Helen Sutherland Yes – that you are striving for something better. Just let me give you this opportunity.

Oliver So I'd be working for you.

Helen Sutherland You'd be working for yourself.

Oliver But what would I owe you?

Helen Sutherland Nothing. It's a gift. You have a gift. I am giving you a gift. What is so difficult about that?

Oliver I dunno, Miss.

Helen Sutherland Look, if it really takes off then you can pay back the money. Please – do this for me.

Oliver For you? What about everyone else?

Helen Sutherland Don't complicate matters. I'm not asking anyone else. This is between me and you.

Oliver But I couldn't just abandon them. We're a group.

Helen Sutherland Nobody's asking you to abandon them. You'll just have time to concentrate on being an artist.

Oliver I just don't know. It's a bit of a shock, Miss. And you're absolutely serious?

Helen Sutherland Of course I'm serious.

Oliver Do you really think I'm good enough?

Helen Sutherland I don't know. But we'll find out. Won't we?

Oliver And you're absolutely serious?

Helen Sutherland Of course I'm serious.

He thinks for some time.

Oliver I don't know what to say. You know no one's ever done anything for me, me entire life, Miss.

Helen Sutherland Well, you should go away and think about it.

Oliver Yes. Of course. I will. Of course, Miss.

Change of scene. Newcastle Central Station. It is night. The guys put on coats and carry tiny overnight cases. They shuffle around in the cold. George takes a register.

George Oliver Kilbourn.

Oliver Yes.

George Harry Wilson.

Harry Yes.

Young Lad Look. I don't understand why you're taking a register. There's only Jimmy missing.

George I know quite nicely that he's missing but we still have to do a register.

Young Lad He's been missing since Ashington.

Harry Where the bloody hell is he?

George We're ganna miss this train if he doesn't hurry himself up.

Oliver You excited, son?

Young Lad I can't believe I'm actually gannin' to London.

Harry Divvint get too excited, you've got a bunk under Jimmy Floyd.

George Where the hell is he?

   Enter Lyon.

Lyon Evening, gentlemen.

George Mr Lyon.

Lyon All present and correct, are we?

Oliver Aye, apart from Jimmy.

George I don't know where the hell he's got to.

Oliver I don't understand. He changed his shift and everything.

Lyon Looking forward to it, Oliver?

Oliver I've not slept for three nights. First the *Listener* article and now this.

Lyon Well, it's terribly good of Miss Sutherland to arrange it. The Chinese Exhibition at the Royal Academy, then the Tate and we've all been invited for tea and madrigals at Jim Ede's in Hampstead, then the train back.

Jimmy comes running in.

Harry Look, here he is.

Jimmy Thank God.

Oliver Where've you been, man?

Jimmy Jack Ainsworth broke his leg on the bottom. By the time we'd got him out I missed the train. I had to hitch-hike off a lorry. I thought there's ne way I was gann get here.

Noise of the steam train in the station.

George Well, howay, or we're ganna miss this one inall.

Harry Coach D.

Jimmy Coach D.

They pick up their bags and start towards Coach D, but Lyon is going in another direction.

Lyon OK – see you later chaps!

George What do you mean? Aren't you coming?

Lyon Of course, but I'm in First Class.

The guys all look in amazement.

Have a good sleep in there. See you in London.

An actor uses a hand-held dry-ice machine to make the effect of steam puffing up and obscuring the guys whilst the whistle blows. During the change of scene the guys lose their coats, and as the 'mist' clears, for the first time the three screens show parts of the same image: a long Chinese painting.

Jimmy They're massive, aren't they?

Harry Apparently this is the largest exhibition of Chinese art ever seen outside China.

Oliver It's funny. It's not what I imagined Chinese paintings to be.

George What did you imagine?

Oliver I don't know – something more Chinese . . . But they're quite simple, aren't they? A bird on a branch, a tree by a stream. I was expecting something more grand.

Young Lad I dunno, I think they're quite grand.

Oliver I meant opulent. They're quite simple, aren't they?

Harry I like them.

George I thought they'd be a bit imperial for you.

Harry No, that's what I like. There's ne posh people in them.

Jimmy They're a bit like them plates, aren't they? With people gannin' across bridges and all that.

Young Lad It's funny, isn't it? The way they don't colour it all in.

George Yer reet. They just leave spaces.

They all look at the picture before them. Lyon walks into the scene as if moving around the exhibition.

Lyon Well, I have to say, it may be two hundred years old, but it really wasn't worth the trouble bringing it over. I don't think there's much evidence of any real skill. Quite clearly generic scenes – perfectly ordinary, really.

Oliver You don't like them?

Lyon There's nothing essentially 'bad' – I just think all this claptrap about spiritual quality is frankly overblown. Don't you think?

Oliver I don't know.

Lyon But there's no demonstration of composition, handling of colour. Compare it with Gainsborough, say, or Stubbs, who was almost directly contemporary. Lovely as it is, it's still really folk art.

Harry What's wrong with folk art?

Lyon Nothing's wrong with folk art *per se*. It's just they are very primitive. Look at the lack of perspective.

Harry But that's what I like about them. They're just things put on. One thing and another – additive painting. That's what a lot of folk art is like, isn't it? No perspective. 'Cos with perspective everyone's looking at everything from one fixed point of view. Whereas if there's not perspective, nothing's fixed – you can come to the painting from wherever you like.

Lyon Well, it's all too specific to be really relevant beyond its immediate circumstances. I just think everybody's too scared to say so.

George I think there's something quite beautiful about it, actually – how it's about everyday thing, simple things and that. Admitedly it's not very similar to Woodhorn Colliery, but it's not that different to what we get up to.

Lyon Well, frankly, I think they're rather formulaic. Look. There are rooms and rooms of this stuff.

Harry Yes – but that's because it's traditional. They're working in a tradition.

Lyon Exactly – there's no individuality. That's precisely what it lacks.

George No – don't be daft. The whole point of a tradition means that every little detail becomes important because every tiny variation within a tradition is a huge mark of individuality.

Oliver You don't have to be wild or eccentric to be individual – you don't have to be different for the sake of it. That's Roger Fry and that whole Omega lot – tradition of the craftsman.

Young Lad Any road, half of the time people are just copying other people being individual – which is not being individual at all, when you think about it.

George The beauty about this is, is that it's traditional and personal. If you use it right, tradition's not something that smothers you – tradition's something that sets you free.

Enter Helen Sutherland.

Lyon Well, Roger Fry aside, I still find it rather limited. What do you think, Helen?

Helen Sutherland I think it's one of the most beautiful things I have ever seen in my life.

The guys smile, knowing they are right. Then this final 'tableau' is broken.

Oliver (*direct address*) And then we went to the Tate Gallery.

A photo of the Tate Gallery appears on the middle screen. Lights go off. We are at a slide show: we see slides of the guys on the steps, and inside examples of the art mentioned.

Harry But the main thing that really impressed us –

George – beyond the Cézannes and Utrillos.

We see Cézannes and Utrillos.

Jimmy I like the Blake.

And a Blake.

George Yeah, we liked the Blake.

Oliver And the Turner.

And a Turner.

George Yes, Turner. That was quite something.

Young Lad And Cézanne.

Oliver We've said Cézanne.

Young Lad Have we?

Harry Basically, we liked everything.

Young Lad Well, nearly everything.

George But the main thing to impress us –

Oliver – the main thing –

Young Lad – was Van Gogh.

Then a self-portrait of Van Gogh.

Oliver Even when we walked into the room. You could feel that this was special.

Harry It might have been the mining connection.

Oliver He used to live in a mining village.

George Before he was a painter.

Jimmy In the Borinage.

A map of the Borinage. Then a picture.

Oliver He was a trainee vicar. Trying to look after the well-being of the miners.

Harry And that's where he learned to draw.

Oliver He was nearly thirty when he started to draw.

More slides of Van Gogh.

George And the first things he actually drew were miners –

Young Lad – coming back from work.

Slides of the early drawings of miners.

Oliver But what seemed overwhelming – was the intensity.

George When you see his room, it's not just like you were in it having a look round –

Harry – it's like you were inside his heed when he was in it.

The slides start coming thick and fast – much more quickly than in any realistic lecture.

George 'I don't paint pictures. I paint experience.' That's what he used to say.

Oliver It's like what Ben Nicholson says: spirituality and painting are the same thing.

Harry And what I liked about the room was that it was an ordinary room – not a rich man's room –

Oliver – not an abstract room.

George It was a vision of the everyday –

Young Lad – but it was more than that.

Jimmy You felt like you were seeing the scene for the first time.

Harry And really, I think it was at that moment –

Jimmy – when we saw the Van Gogh. Something happened.

Oliver When we saw the Van Gogh I think –

George – we became a group.

Oliver Because we saw art was not about the privileged.

George It wasn't about money.

Harry Or doing things a right way or a wrong way.

George Art was a gift –

Oliver – a vision –

Jimmy – we all have, one way or another.

Oliver It was about living.

George Some of us to paint.

Jimmy Others of us to look, and see.

Young Lad Art was about how you live your life.

Oliver And it is to be cherished.

Harry And it is to be shared. Art doesn't really belong to anybody.

Jimmy Not the artist.

Harry Or the owner.

Jimmy Or the people who look at it.

Oliver Real art is something shared –

Harry – power that's shared.

Young Lad Real art belongs to everyone.

Harry And when we looked at the picture –

Now we are on the Van Gogh of the room with a vase full of flowers. We flick through more slides and we see details, huge close-ups as they flick by.

Oliver – we felt a force. The force that flowed through the flower – flowed through us.

George You could actually feel it.

Jimmy Something he had done.

George We were feeling it, as one.

Harry You might call it spirituality –

Oliver – or religion or creativity or energy –

Harry – or inspiration.

Oliver Yes.

George And we could feel it.

Oliver 'Cos he'd captured that energy –

Young Lad – of being alive.

Oliver It was an inspiration –

Harry – and that's what 'inspired' means. Doesn't it?

Oliver Breathing life.

George When yer inspired – it means seeing clearly how to capture that energy.

Jimmy It means knaaing what to de.

Oliver You see what is there. And you see what is possible.

The slides should be coming thick and fast. Maybe they are great works of art contrasted with great works of struggle, but they should be moving and emotional images, and finally images from the group.

73

Jimmy You can take one set of things –

George – some board, some paint, whatever.

Jimmy You can take this one set of things –

Oliver – and you can make them something else.

Harry Whatever your circumstances –

Young Lad – rich or poor.

Jimmy And you make them something else.

Oliver This is what art shows you.

George No matter how hard or how easy.

Oliver You can take things.

George And transform them.

Harry You don't have to put up with what you're given.

Jimmy And not just into anything.

George You can transform things and make something beautiful –

Jimmy – something profound.

George You can make something –

Jimmy – that's the work of art –

Harry – that you can change things.

Oliver And you can overcome whatever you need to overcome.

Harry No matter who you are, where you come from.

Oliver You need a brush –

Jimmy – or whatever –

Oliver – canvas or bit of old card –

Young Lad – and change things.

74

Harry And that is what is important about art.

Jimmy You take one thing –

George – and you make one thing into another –

Oliver – and you transform – who you are.

The slide show is finished. The group are caught in the 'headlights' of the slide projector. They are looking out into the audience. In contrast to their high-flown rhetoric, they look vulnerable. They stare out uncertainly.
  Blackout.

End of Act One.

Act Two

Projection:

THE HUT: THE COMMITTEE MEETING

A projection of Oliver's picture of the committee meeting. George, the Young Lad, Harry, Jimmy, Lyon and Oliver are sitting round a horseshoe of tables.

George A stipend.

Lyon A stipend?!

Oliver Yes, a stipend.

Jimmy What the bloody hell's a stipend?

Lyon It's a sort of regular payment.

Oliver Like a wage.

Jimmy A wage?

George What for?

Oliver Painting.

Young Lad Painting!

Jimmy She'll give you a wage for painting?!

Oliver Yes.

George How much did she offer exactly?

Oliver Two quid.

Jimmy Two quid –

Oliver And ten shillings. Basically what I get at the pit.

George Every week?

Jimmy She didn't mention me by any chance?

George Of course she didn't mention ye, yer lucky to get paid doon the pit never mind painting bloody pictures.

Jimmy What you on aboot, it's mine she's got up in the hoose.

George Anyway, I don't see why you're getting so aereated – ye divvint even want to be an artist.

Jimmy I wouldn't mind the two quid, though.

Young Lad And she'll just give you this money to give up working?

Oliver Yes.

Young Lad For nowt?

Oliver Well, to paint –

Young Lad Why would she do that?

Oliver She's trying to help me.

Young Lad By becoming a painter?

Oliver I wasn't gonna say anything, but I've not been able to stop thinking about it. I'm asking for help here.

George Well, you've picked a fine bloody time to bring this up – we're supposed to be preparing for the exhibition.

Harry And she'd give you this money every week?

Oliver Yes.

Jimmy Well, there's ne accounting for taste.

Young Lad So it'd be like retiring?

Harry Of course it wouldn't be like retiring – he'd have to work as an artist, wouldn't he?

Young Lad Well, how do you do that?

Harry What do you think – you paint pictures.

Young Lad Every day?

George Of course every day, it'd be like a job.

Oliver Just like any other artist, that's the whole point.

Jimmy But you'll run oota things to draw.

George Course he won't run out of things to draw, he'll have all day to think about it.

Jimmy What if she changes her mind?

George She's not gonna change her mind.

Jimmy She might run out of money.

Harry She's one of the richest people in the country, man. She's not ganna run out of money.

George So it's like charity.

Young Lad Patronage, actually.

George Shut up, you. But that's the problem, isn't it? You'd be in her pay.

Harry He's in somebody's pay noo – he's happy taking money off the Duke of Portland.

George I knaa, but this is different? He'd be compromised, wouldn't he?

Jimmy Well, he's compromised now, isn't he, 'cos he's working doon a pit all day.

Oliver Anyway, she says I can paint what I like.

Jimmy Aye, she says that noo, but she'll have you on circles and squares before you can say Al Jolson, mark my words.

Harry And she'd keep all the paintings.

Oliver No, I'd sell the paintings. You have to see the stipend as sort a gift.

Jimmy Well, I just divvint think it's fair.

Young Lad What do you mean, it isn't fair?

Jimmy On us. You could always share it oot, I suppose.

Harry How's he ganna share it out? It's for him to live on, you stupid sod.

Jimmy But yer right, I divvint see how you can take it. He'd be an outsider, wouldn't he?

Harry What do you mean?

Jimmy Well, he'd be like a scab.

Oliver Hey!

Harry What do you mean, a scab?

Jimmy Well, we'd all be doing one thing and he'd be doing another. Look, nebody's an artist round here. Aye, we might do art, 'cos of this art class, but we do it as a group, we do it as equals. Now if somebody is going to break ranks and get two pund and ten shilling a week and others are gonna get sweet bugger-all for their labours, I'd say there's a basic inequality there, not two million miles away from being a blackleg.

Harry That's got nowt to do with being a scab. A scab is someone who's undermining everybody else. What would he be undermining by painting pictures, you stupid sod?

Lyon Gentlemen, please!

79

Jimmy I thought we were supposed be a group here. I thought this was a common enterprise.

Lyon So what do you think, Oliver?

Oliver I don't know. I can't see anything clearly any more. I've never had nebody to tell uz what to de. I just had to do it meself. But this time – I just divvint knaa. Look – when I sit doon to draw something, it's new. It's always a struggle, but in the end I make something; and I might spend a day doon the pit, I like being doon the pit, when I come out I've made a bit of money, but when I've painted a picture, I've made a bit of art. Something special in the world, ye knaa, unique. And I think what I could achieve if I spent that time every day. I think of how I could grow. What I could become.

Young Lad But you can't give up a job. Not a pit job. Not you, Mr Kilbourn. You've got twenty-five years left. Do you know how hard it is to get a job as a pitman? Yer sorted. It's a job for life. How could you even think of packing that in? The laddie's reet. And anyway, how ye ganna be an artist roond here? What ye ganna de, gan roond with a beret?

George Don't be bloody stupid, Jimmy. So are you gonna take it, Oliver?

Oliver I divvint knaa what to do.

Jimmy All those in favour.

George Hang on a minute. This is not something we're gonna sort out now. So if there's ne further business, I think we should reconvene at the gallery.

The group get up and start putting their coats on. Oliver is still sitting, pondering his position. Lyon comes up to him as the others leave.

Oliver What do you think, Mr Lyon?

Lyon It's a very difficult decision. It's obviously quite an opportunity. I mean, the whole thing has come as a bit of a shock to me, to tell you the truth. But being a Sunday painter, so to speak, is a very different prospect from being a full-time professional artist. What you have to realise is that what you have here is very, very special. The creative environment, working in consort with others, the guidance, our relationship. These are very special things, Oliver – you don't find them very easily. Everything you – all these decisions – determine what kind of artist you are. Nobody can really decide any of this other than yourself. You are a very special person to me, Oliver, and I want you to know whatever you decide I will be right there for you.

Lyon leaves. Harry has been sitting at the back, listening, almost invisible.

Harry Take it. Take it. For God's sake. Paint. You were born to it. If you were one of them you'd have the choice, wouldn't you?

George Are you serious, Harry? You divvint think it's selling out?

Harry Selling out? Two quid a week – those bastards owe us millions. Look at all the paintings we saw. You tell me which ones were paid for and which ones weren't. You can't tell. Money doesn't buy you art, money buys you time. 'Man makes his own history but not in conditions of his own making' – Karl Marx. What are you doing, slaving down there every day? I'd give me right arm to jack my job in. Do it. Don't listen to them. You might not be the best painter here. But if any of we could make a go of it, it's you, Oliver. People like you. You've got no ties. A job in a pit? You might be crippled tomorrow. Bugger what anybody else thinks. Take it. Think about it as a redistribution of wealth.

Change of scene. The usual loud noise. but this time it is the sharp baying of an audience at a gallery. The chitter-chatter is as aggressive and abrasive as the industrial noises in the first half.

The projection shows we are at the the group's first exhibition, Bensham, Gateshead, 1938.

Jimmy Can you believe how many people there are?

George Half of them have come up from London, ye knaa.

Harry Mind, have you seen the plight of them surrealists? They want a bloody good wash.

Oliver What's that?

George A crate of beer.

Oliver Ye divvint even drink.

George I knaa, it's from that stupid sod who stayed at wor hoose.

Harry Not the one from Oxford University.

George Aye, he left it as a present. Buggered off without paying any board. They divvint knaa how to gan on, son.

Harry What ye ganna de with it?

George I divvint knaa.

Young Lad I'll have some.

George No you will not. Alcohol – it's a thief of time, man. You should have seen the sod, running roond the landing in bits of rags. They divvint even have pyjamas, man.

Enter Lyon.

Lyon Well, I think it's quite a success. Julian Trevelyan is absolutely knocked out. He's definitely going to buy something.

Harry One of mine?

Lyon He's not quite sure yet. And there's someone from the BBC who has asked us to give a talk on the wireless.

Jimmy On the radio . . .

Lyon He's asked me to pick one or two of you to go with me to the place on New Bridge Street to talk about what we're doing.

Young Lad That's amazing.

Jimmy I'll gan.

George No you won't. Nebody'll understand you.

Lyon I don't think this is the time to discuss this. We should be starting the discussion. But I just want to say: jolly well done, chaps, this is a proper achievement.

The scene changes. Lyon is addressing the audience. Behind him a series of images of the work of the Ashington Group are projected.

Lyon What is remarkable about these pictures is not the quality or quantity of the work but the fact that it exists at all. What you are seeing before you is perhaps unique in the history of art. There have often been individuals to break out – balk expectations – but I can think of no other group of working people who have created such a body of art. And to me it begs the question: why should we assume that art is the exclusive domain of the educated, the privileged, the elite? Why do we assume these people have more to say than anyone else? And here is the lie to that assumption. Here is the evidence that as a society we have got it wrong, and in every mine, every street, workplace, is the potential for works of art to blossom and grow and amaze us with their riches. I know I am not alone in finding these works exceptional. But they are only as exceptional as the men who have made them. This is the first exhibition of paintings entirely by working-class artists in British history. The reason why we have not seen its like before, is clearly not because the working class lack talent, but because no one has given them a paintbrush.

Lights come up on the gallery.

And what this all offers to me is the fact that anyone can paint. You simply have to find the key and unlock all this creativity, which as a society we have hitherto allowed to lie dormant. Ladies and gentlemen – the Ashington Group.

Polite applause.

Would anybody like to say anything?

Lyon sits down. A pause. Oliver stands up.

Oliver Oliver Kilbourn, miner. I just want to say: that's not quite right, is it?

Harry What do you mean?

Oliver It's not right. I don't think that's right.

Harry You can't just say that. You have to explain why.

Oliver Wey, it's obvious, isn't it? Some people can paint and other people can't.

Harry But I think he's saying that the creativity of the mass of people has been stymied by the workings of capitalism, but essentially everybody has a creative gift.

Lyon I'm not quite saying that exactly.

Harry But it's true – basic division of labour – whole sections of society are excluded from something which is an inalienable human right. Surely you have to agree with that.

Oliver But we're not excluded – we're doing it, aren't we?

Lyon Exactly – you are the exception that proves the rule.

Oliver But that's not the same as saying everyone can paint, is it?

Jimmy True – wor lass can't paint.

George Neither can ye.

Lyon But look – you are celebrated all over the country. There are, what, fifty people here from London because you can paint.

Oliver Aye – that's 'cos we're good at it.

Lyon But you are ordinary people who are good at it.

Oliver Exactly – if everybody was good at it nebody would be interested, would they? That's the whole point of art. Art is valued because it's special – exceptional. That's the whole point, man, Harry.

Harry But what I'm saying is that everybody is exceptional.

Oliver I mean some people are good at things and others are not. I mean some fellas grow leeks, some fellas can run the length of a pitch and lob a ball ower three defenders' heeds smack in the corner of the net. It's individual talent, isn't it? You'd have to agree with that, Harry.

Lyon But art is different – because art is about expressing yourself.

Oliver Art is about doing good pictures.

Jimmy I agree.

Lyon The question seems to me: who defines good and bad?

Oliver It doesn't matter who defines good and bad. When I sit down to de a painting I don't sit down to do a bad one or a mediocre one – I sit down to do something good. I'm not expressing meself if I do a bad picture – it's obvious.

Lyon But just 'cos a picture isn't excellent does not stop it from being art.

Harry But everything we do is art – art is the way we move, art is the things we say, art is the choices we make in an effort to express who we are.

George So now you're saying everything is art?!

Harry Yes. Human labour – creation of value – what's the difference between howking out a bit of coal and howking out a sculpture – it's fundamentally the same thing.

Jimmy That's absolutely ridiculous. You waddn't put a bit of coal on yer mantelpiece.

Oliver Anybody can cut oot a bit of coal – not everybody can make a sculpture.

George Not everybody can cut oot coal.

Oliver There you gan. Everybody is not equal. Some people are good at stuff and other people are not. If we were posh people nebody would be saying, 'Look at this – all posh people are artists,' would they? We didn't need posh people helping, we did this worselves.

George What about Mr Lyon?

Jimmy He was more of a hindrance, if you ask me.

George What about the group?

Oliver But isn't what matters about art that it comes from an individual person? It's somebody's life, somebody's journey. Isn't that what's important?

Harry Anyway, we are individuals. There's twenty-five thousand people in Ashington. We just happen to be the ones who can paint.

Oliver I don't want to make a big deal of it. All I am saying is, it's easy for people from the outside to see us as a bunch of miners. But we don't see ourselves as that – we see ourselves as individuals, don't we?

Lyon Of course. But what is interesting is the way you all paint the same things. You have a common objective, a shared experience. This is very special.

Harry What do you expect – we're all from the same place, aren't we?

Oliver I know you don't mean it badly or anything, Mr Lyon. I do understand what you're saying, but I think you have to be careful, don't you – the assumptions you make – that they don't actually end up patronising people or holding people back.

Lyon That's the last thing anyone would want to do.

Jimmy Can I get this right, Oliver – so, basically, all you're really saying is most people can't paint?

Harry For chrissakes, he's saying – everybody has their own journey. Is there anything wrong with that?

Everybody rearranges the stage around Oliver, who is standing awkwardly in the middle of the stage. He puts on bicycle clips and a cap to be ready for the next scene.

When the scene is set, projections tell us we are back at Rock Hall. Oliver is on his own, looking decidedly nervous. Suddenly there is a voice from nowhere:

Ben Nicholson Hello.

Oliver gets a shock. He has not noticed.

Oliver Hello.

Ben Nicholson Come to see Her Ladyship.

Oliver Yes. They told me just to wait in here.

Ben Nicholson Having one of her naps. Very fond of naps. A smoke?

Oliver Are we allowed?

Ben Nicholson Don't worry about it. Blame it on me.

Ben lights the cigarette. He gives it to Oliver.

Ben. Ben Nicholson.

Oliver The artist?

Ben Nicholson The dogsbody of the *nouveaux riches* – or at least their superannuated daughters. So it appears.

Oliver I beg your pardon.

Ben Nicholson Sorry, I've just been up here too long. This weather. Can't even get out – I've not had a normal conversation for days. Are you doing some work on the house?

Oliver Not exactly. I've come up to talk to Miss Sutherland. Actually, I'm a great admirer of yours.

Ben Nicholson Really!

Oliver Yes, especially the more abstract work.

Ben Nicholson Goodness!

Oliver Oh aye, I couldn't get it at first. But now I really admire it.

Ben Nicholson Well, thank you.

It dawns on him.

You're not one of the miners, are you?

Oliver Actually, yes, I am.

Ben Nicholson Incredible. We went to see your exhibition yesterday. It's really incredible.

Oliver Thank you.

Ben Nicholson No, really. I was amazed. She's prone to exaggerate her new finds, but I was properly impressed. We all were. Are you staying for supper?

Oliver No. No. I just cycled up. I have to be back in a bit. I'm on nights.

Ben Nicholson Just as well really. It's a bit like boarding school. My advice: avoid all comestibles. She has a witch from the village who provides infinite varieties of indigestible stodge, very big on suet.

Oliver You come here a lot, don't you?

Ben Nicholson All part of the gig really. Keeping the customers satisfied. To be quite honest, it's all right till she gets out the William Blake. Be warned. Then you really are in trouble. But it has to be done – it's pretty tough out there. We're on the brink of war. I have to say that's what I envy about you chaps.

Oliver What's that?

Ben Nicholson No patrons, no public, no press. You're free, aren't you? You've got it made. It's what we're trying to do at St Ives. A shared aesthetic, a community of makers, but it can never be what you have. You can't recreate something like that. You can see it in the work. You didn't do the one of the whippet by any chance?

Oliver No, no. That was, somebody else – I do a lot of stuff of working underground.

Ben Nicholson Brilliant. Really exceptional.

Oliver If you don't mind me asking, how did you start off being an artist, Mr Nicholson?

Ben Nicholson Family trade, I suppose. Daddy was an artist, so I didn't really think of anything else. Unfortunately he ran off with my fiancée just when I left the Slade, so I've pretty much had to find my own way.

Oliver Oh. I see.

Ben Nicholson It was pretty tough at first. I bummed about Europe – that's where I first met Braque and Giacometti. Didn't sell very much for the first ten years or so – mostly lived off Winifred's inheritence – but that's rather dried up since I moved in with Barbara.

Oliver Barbara?

Ben Nicholson Hepworth.

Oliver You live with Barbara Hepworth?!

Ben Nicholson For my sins. We haven't got two sous to rub together, so I've started taking on pupils and eating a lot of stodgy suppers, shall we say.

Oliver So you just come here so you can sell work?

Ben Nicholson Oh, she's all right, really. A bit stuck up her own arse. But it's just part of the aftercare service. I suppose that's what I admire most about you guys.

Oliver I don't understand.

Ben Nicholson You are your own men. You can't be bought.

Enter Helen Sutherland.

Helen Sutherland Oliver!

Ben Nicholson I'll leave you to it.

Helen Sutherland No, Ben, please stay.

Ben Nicholson No, Helen, darling. I was just on my way to freshen up. Frightfully good to meet you. Jolly good luck.

Helen Sutherland It's very good of you to come up here, Oliver.

Oliver It's the least I could do in the circumstances.

Helen Sutherland I see you met Ben. He's a sweetheart, isn't he?

Oliver I can't believe I actually met him.

Helen Sutherland I hear the exhibition went very well. Did you sell anything?

Oliver One piece. Though Jimmy made us a fortune. But it was nice just to be shown in a proper gallery.

Helen Sutherland Personally, I'm not sure being in the public eye is such a good thing for an artist. The most important thing is staying focused on the work.

Oliver Well, Mr Lyon is very good at getting us noticed.

Helen Sutherland Mr Lyon is very good at getting himself noticed. So . . . have you thought about my offer?

Oliver To be quite honest, I haven't thought about anything else. You're sure about it?

Helen Sutherland Of course I'm sure.

Oliver Well, obviously I've given it a lot of thought. I mean, it's not every day you get an offer like this, and it's a big decision. I mean, I want to get this right, and I've given this a lot of thought, talked to a lot of people, I mean, it's not just me this is ganna affect. Such a big step and everything. So I've weighed everything up, all the pros and cons.

Helen Sutherland And?

Pause.

Oliver The answer's no, Miss.

Helen Sutherland No?!

Oliver Yes, no. I'm sorry, Miss.

Helen Sutherland Are you sure about this?

Oliver Yes, I am.

Helen Sutherland Perhaps you need more time. It's such a big change.

Oliver No, Miss.

Helen Sutherland You do realise what an unusual offer this is, Oliver?

Oliver Of course I do. But I have no choice, Miss. I know you've been very kind and everything, but I couldn't do that. Become an artist.

Helen Sutherland Why not, Oliver?

Oliver I just can't. How could I give up me job? How could I cut meself off from everybody?

Helen Sutherland Nobody's asking you to cut yourself off.

Oliver It's not as simple as that. What if you change your mind?

Helen Sutherland I'm not going to change my mind.

Oliver It's not about me. It's about everybody else.

Helen Sutherland Don't be stupid. They would take my hand off if it were them. You know that.

Oliver But it might not work.

Helen Sutherland What if it did?

Oliver You don't understand. It's not just a job. I'd be giving up everything.

Helen Sutherland You're not giving up anything – you'd just become an artist. Like everybody else.

Oliver 'Like everybody else'?!

Helen Sutherland Like whomever you wanted to be. That's the point. You make it up. You decide who you are. You've got no ties, Oliver.

Oliver You don't have a clue, do you?

Helen Sutherland Yes, I know exactly. You're scared, Oliver. You're all the same. Take your life in your own hands for once. Look, it's not your fault you had a crippled father, it's not your fault you had a mother who abandoned you, it's not your fault you're working-class, that you were born here. But you can't let that define you. Redefine yourself – don't just accept some secondhand version.

Oliver 'Scared'? You gotta be joking. I get scared down the pit. I'm not scared of painting. It's not that. It's that I haven't got the language. I am who I am. You can't be an artist and be working-class. It doesn't exist. I'd have to be something else.

Helen Sutherland And what the hell's wrong with that?

Oliver I've known those blokes since I was a kid, Miss, as far back as I can remember. I knaa their fathers and their kids, they've pulled iz oot of the pit, they've looked after me sister, these people are like a family to me. They are my family – they are everything I've got. I'm not me on me own. You can go off and find any number of people just like you. Well, I can't. It's not as simple for me.

Helen Sutherland Listen to you, Oliver, for God's sake. Don't be pathetic. I'm throwing you a lifeline here.

Oliver So I just give everything up. Because you graciously decide to pluck me out. No – it doesn't work like that. You can't just change who people are by throwing money at them. It's not just about the money, it's about everything else. It's about who people are. It's about how I think, about how I feel. How I do everything I do. Yes, of course you can get out if you're a bairn. But it's too late – I'm never gonna be like you. You are 'them' – I'm a pitman, and a bloody good pitman.

The scene breaks.

Sounds of war. A slide shows:

1939

THE GROUP AT WAR – THE HUT

Then lights come up. Jimmy is standing centre stage with an abstract picture, carefully painted. They stare at it.

George What the hell is that?

Jimmy It's an experiment.

George I can see it's an experiment, but what the hell is it supposed to be?

Jimmy It's a blob.

Harry A blob?

Oliver Has it got a name, though?

Jimmy Yes, I call it 'The Blob'.

George It's a load of bloody rubbish.

Jimmy No, it's not. That's non-representational art, that is.

Harry But it's just a blob.

Jimmy Exactly.

Oliver I thought we were trying to do 'Preparations for Battle'. For the War Ministry.

Jimmy Aye, well, this is 'Preparations for Battle' – in the form of a blob.

George What do you mean, it's 'Preparations for Battle'? It's got nothing to do with preparations for battle.

Jimmy It might not to you. But to me this says: anticipation, war, approaching atrocities, the lot.

Harry It's got nothing to do with war or approaching atrocities – it is just a blob.

Jimmy Aye, well, that's because it's non-representational.

Oliver I thought we were supposed to be doing something for the War Ministry. They're not gonna have that up, are they?

Jimmy I divvint see what's wrang with it. Every bugger else is deing blobs – left, right and centre.

Lyon Look, I think what Oliver is saying is, that whilst it may be a blob, and it may be non-representational, it's not really coming from 'you'.

Jimmy Where else is it coming from? Hey, I dragged this up from my subconscious on the allotment during an air raid, for chrissakes. Oh, it's all right if Picasso does

a blob, or some posh bloke from London does a blob –
but when I de one, it 'doesn't come from me'.

George It doesn't really matter. Whoever painted it, it
would still be rubbish. They're never ganna put that up.

Jimmy So all blobs are rubbish, are they? What if Henry
Moore did a blob, would that be rubbish inall?

George If that's the one he did – yes!

Harry Look, nebody's saying all blobs are rubbish.
Obviously there are blobs and blobs. There were perfectly
fine blobs in the Russian Revolution, for example. The
trouble is, this one doesn't mean anything.

Jimmy What do you mean, it 'doesn't mean anything'?
That's the whole point. It's challenging the very modes of
representation.

Harry Where's he learnt this?

Jimmy I can read, ye knaa.

Oliver But why are you challenging the modes of
representation? What's so wrang with representation all
of a sudden?

Jimmy That's what I'm saying, man, it's all old hat. Ye
divvint think yer modern artists in London are deing
people in Anderson shelters and stuff like that? Wey no,
man, they're challenging the modes of representation.

Oliver Aye, but they're proper artists, aren't they, that's
what they de – art. Their job is to think about the way
you can represent things. It's all they de. But we're not
full-time artists so it doesn't mean the same thing. We are
involved in other things, so us doing art means something
different.

Jimmy Why's it different for us?

Harry Because we divvint have the means of representation in the first place – how things are represented doesn't belong to the working class at all. That's exactly what we have to take back. And this is tantamount to bourgeois formalism.

Jimmy How the hell's this bourgeois formalism? I did it on the allotment.

Harry It doesn't matter where you did it. It doesn't mean anything because it isn't involved in a proper aesthetic question addressing the class basis of its means of production.

George So you are saying all blobs are rubbish.

Harry No, I'm saying if someone else was deing a blob – Barbara Hepworth, for instance – she'd be deing a blob in reaction to whatever other artists were deing. Her blob might be a revolutionary blob for all I know, because she'd be attacking the bourgeois ideology of the current art world. But your blob is just mimicking a style which is actually somebody else's. It's like doffing yer cap to the Lord of the Manor.

Jimmy So if I can't de blobs, what am I allowed to draw?

Oliver He's right, there can't be one lot of things that posh people can draw and another lot of things for us.

Harry Yes, that is what I'm saying. It's got to be right. Some things are bound to be more relevant. Look, if I paint a picture of the Duke of bloody Portland it's gonna have a different feel than if some sod comes up from the Royal Academy. We've all got different points of view. It's still the same subject, isn't it? But one's reactionary and one's a politicised piece of art.

Jimmy You're the bloody reactionary.

George Enough.

Lyon Look, I think the problem with your blob is that neither the form nor the subject really express very much. It's just an ugly blob – a graphic image on a piece of paper. An elaborately painted doodle. It has no resonance. The point is, even abstract art must capture the inner beauty of something to be effective.

Jimmy What's beautiful about his?

We see Harry's picture of 'The War Wedding'.

It's not even about war.

George Of course it's about war. Look, that lad's in a uniform.

Jimmy But it's on the High Street.

Oliver But that's the whole point. It's about us, it's not some abstraction – it's not about war elsewhere, it's about some young lad gannin' off.

Jimmy I still divvint see what's beautiful about it.

Lyon It's about the fragility of things. That's what good art's about, isn't it? Capturing moments of real fragility that in life pass by but in art we are reminded of them. Reminded of mortality.

Jimmy What, outside of Woolworth's?

Oliver Anywhere.

Jimmy Exactly, it's just depressing. We should be inspiring people to fight fascism, not reminding them of mortality. And look at that, man, what's that supposed to be?

Oliver It's of a blackout.

Jimmy You cannit see anything.

Oliver That's the point.

Jimmy But there's nothing beautiful about a blackout.

Young Lad Do you actually listen to yourself? Do yous actually think about what yous are saying? It's crap. It's all sentimental rubbish, man. Blobs, blokes down the High Street – give me a break, man. Real artists would be tearing the whole lot up. Do yous knaa what's gannin' on?

George What on earth are you going on about?

Young Lad We're at war, man. People are being blown to little bits. Whole towns are getting smashed to the ground. And what are we deing? Arguing about art.

Harry So you think we should just give up, do ye? Oh that's reet, let the philistines win.

Young Lad Wey, as it happens, Hitler's an artist and Churchill's an artist. So where does that get you? And I'll tell yous what – they're crap inall. Look.

Harry What's that?

Young Lad I found it in a magazine.

Over the three screens a triptych of 'Guernica' comes up.

George Where've ye been getting money for magazines?

Young Lad In the library.

George You mean you ripped it oot?

Young Lad They wouldn't let uz borrow it.

George You little sod, you'll glue this back in.

Oliver Who did this?

Young Lad It's Picasso, isn't it?

Oliver It's brilliant.

Young Lad Look at it. That's proper art. That's aboot war. Everything ripped up, stuff stuck together, not white boxes or folks on their lunch break. It's people getting killed.

Harry It's alreet for all them cubists swanning around in Paris. 'Slumming it'! He wants to get ower here. I'll show him slumming it.

Jimmy Anyway, I divvint see what's beautiful about that.

Young Lad It isn't beautiful. It's horrible. It's ugly and disgusting. You're scared. All of yous are scared of the big things – tappy-lappying around with yer cushy little jobs, happy as fucking sandboys. If ye's were in Russia they'd have you shipped off to Siberia.

Harry Where do you think we are, son?

Young Lad Well, show uz. Where's the anger in this? Where's the fucking anger?

Change of scene. The stage is cleared and a sign says:

LAING ART GALLERY EXHIBITION, 1941

We see more images painted by the group on the three screens. The lads run in with sandwiches.

Jimmy Here, stick these in yer pocket. George is getting the pork pie.

George I've got it.

The Young Lad comes in.

Where the hell have you been?

Young Lad Have I missed anything?

Jimmy Yer alreet – there's neone here, son.

George That's besides the point. You were supposed to be here to help set up. I should've banned ye when I had the chance.

Young Lad I'm sorry, Uncle George, I got a bit held up at the station.

George Have ye been drinking, lad?

Young Lad No.

George You stink of alcohol, son.

Young Lad I've only had a pint of beer.

George For chrisssakes, are you surprised you divvint get work with that attitude?

Young Lad Well, it won't matter any more. I've signed up.

Oliver You did what?

Young Lad I was in the station and I got talking to these lads with a stall.

George For God's sake, son, what are you thinking of?

Young Lad It's alreet, I would've got conscripted anyway.

Harry Divvint be stupid, mining's a prescribed occupation, son.

Young Lad In case you hadn't noticed, I'm not a miner, am I? I'm a nebody.

Oliver But there'll be plenty of work now it's all kicking in.

Jimmy Look, it's not too late. I'll gan with yer uncle and we'll sort it oot, son.

Young Lad No. Ye's divvint get it, de ye? I want to gan. They were glad to have uz. They didn't look down on uz.

George Jesus Christ. Did you think of your poor mother?

Young Lad Stuff it. Stuff the lot of yous. I'm getting out of here. You can keep yer dirty, stinking slagheaps.

George Come back here!

As the Young Lad storms off, Helen Sutherland swans through.

Oh, Miss Sutherland.

Helen Sutherland Lads.

Jimmy Would you care for a sausage roll?

Helen Sutherland No, thank you.

Jimmy Cucumber sandwich? They're very nice.

Helen Sutherland Really. I ate before I came.

George Well, it's a great privilege that you came, Miss.

Oliver We're a bit disappointed at the turnout.

Jimmy Though they've put a very good spread on.

Helen Sutherland I was surprised at the numbers myself. I suppose war makes philistines of a lot of people.

Jimmy At least we'll be able to take most of this hyem. Are you sure about the sausage roll?

George So have you seen anything you like, Miss?

Helen Sutherland To be quite honest, I've pretty much given up on painting altogether. I get most excited by ceramics, actually.

Jimmy What, plates and that?

George Shut it.

Helen Sutherland There are some lovely things coming out of St Ives.

George That's a shame, we could de with the money. Things are a bit short, you know.

Helen Sutherland Don't worry, that's why I brought Lady Ridley – more money than sense, always ten years behind the times. She'll lap it up, believe me. Is this one of yours, Oliver?

Helen leads Oliver downstage and they stare out, looking at Oliver's painting, which appears on a screen behind them.

Oliver Yeah, it's one I did for the War Ministry. George got a grant. That's why it has a war theme.

Helen Sutherland I see.

Oliver Though we've obviously had a lot of guidance from Mr Lyon, of course.

Helen Sutherland Of course.

Oliver So what do you think, Miss?

Helen Sutherland Of this?

Oliver Of my work as a whole.

Helen Sutherland To be quite frank, Oliver, I am a little disappointed.

Oliver Disappointed?

Helen Sutherland I really thought you might have come on a little more than you seem to.

Oliver How do you mean?

Helen Sutherland You know, when we talked, I thought perhaps I was wrong, perhaps you'd have more actual independence by going your own way, by being outside of the 'establishment' as you say. Being more 'individual'. But it's all so generic, Oliver. It's strangely the same as everybody else. You just repeat yourselves, painting the same things, there's no development. I mean, they are all fine, Oliver, but you haven't grown.

Oliver I'm sorry you think that.

Helen Sutherland I shouldn't have been so forthright. I just don't want to patronise you.

Oliver No, you're right, speak your mind.

Helen Sutherland Well, I think what characterises your work is true of the group as a whole. The strange thing is, although you don't deal in sentiment, I think your work ends up being sentimental in the end.

Oliver Really?

Helen Sutherland The fact that you don't really deal with 'form'. That your obsessions really just tell half of a story. For a group of men – there is no sex in your paintings. There's barely anything sublimated. There are hardly any women – but more than that, one doesn't feel 'desire' in the work at all.

Oliver What do you mean, 'desire'?

Helen Sutherland An elemental hunger. The yearning for the other, for sensuality – it's all locked in. It's all conforming. I think that's what you need to work on. It's all there inside you, Oliver, you have to let it out.

Oliver So you don't really like them?

Helen Sutherland No. I'm sure it sounds bitter and somehow related to being rejected, etcetera – maybe it is, but it's truly what I think.

Oliver I feel a bit bad I never came up to paint in the garden like you offered. It's been very difficult, you know, finding time and that. Maybe I could come up one Sunday.

Helen Sutherland Didn't Robert tell you? I'm selling up.

Oliver Oh.

Helen Sutherland It's just too much, up there on my own. Impossible to get anyone up from London.

Oliver But where will you go?

Helen Sutherland I don't know, as yet. I was thinking about a complete fresh start – maybe building somewhere new in the Lakes. But we'll see.

Oliver But you're taking the paintings, though.

Helen Sutherland Of course. The Nicholsons are starting to fetch some very handsome prices.

Oliver I should have taken it, shouldn't I, Miss?

Helen Sutherland I don't know, Oliver – with everything that's happened . . . I think I should go and attend to Lady Ridley.

Susan Hello.

Harry Hello.

Susan Don't you remember me? I came up to your hut, to do some modelling.

Harry Yes, of course. Jimmy still gets palpitations.

Jimmy Yer not thinking of getting yer cleys off in here, are you?

Susan No, I came to see the exhibition. I didn't realise yous were famous.

Harry Who?

Susan Yous.

Oliver We're not famous, pet.

Susan Well, you've got an exhibition at the Laing Art Gallery.

Jimmy And we had one in London, inall.

Harry Hardly a great success, though.

Jimmy Just 'cos ye didn't sell any paintings.

Susan You're very well known in the art world. I think they're great.

Jimmy We de wer best, ye knaa – we never got a proper training like you did.

Oliver I suppose you're a professional by now.

Susan No – I never actually finished. The juggling was too much.

George Christ! Ye never de that as well?!

Susan Too many jobs. Now I just work in the tearoom.

Jimmy But do you still take yer clothes off?

Susan Not since I got engaged – me fiancé didn't like it. But I'm still very interested in the arts, though. It must be the best thing in the world to do what you do. I'd love to be in an exhibition.

The Young Lad comes in with a sherry.

Young Lad Hello.

Susan Hello.

Jimmy After the first one they get a bit boring, to be honest.

Harry The novelty's worn off – especially with the war on.

Susan It can't be that bad. That's Lady Ridley over there. Apparently she's got a massive art collection.

Young Lad She's got a massive arse on her, inall.

Oliver Do you manage to do any painting yerself, then?

Susan I haven't got the time. But maybes after the war's over I'll go back and do a few lessons. Mr Lyon –

Lyon Sorry?

Susan First year. I was in Alexander Thompson's class. Susan Parks. Life model.

Lyon Oh of course, Susan, I didn't recognise you with . . . How delightful to see you. You've changed.

Susan Well, I've put a bit of weight on.

Lyon No, I don't think so. It's just . . . How lovely to see you. I'm a bit distracted, I'm afraid. I've had some extraordinary news.

George Really?

Lyon Yes, actually. That's why I'm late. I've just come from the University. I received a telegram just as I was coming down here.

Jimmy Would you care for a sandwich?

Lyon No, thank you.

Jimmy Scotch egg?

George Jimmy, for chrissakes.

Lyon I've just been appointed the Professor at the Edinburgh College of Art.

Oliver Edinburgh.

Lyon It's the sort of Scottish equivalent of the Royal Academy.

Susan That's fantastic.

Young Lad Well done, mate.

George Shut up.

Lyon To be quite honest, it's an extraordinary appointment for someone with my background. I think to be honest it's all down to you chaps.

Harry Us?

Lyon Yes, I think the dissertation swung it.

George Dissertation?

Lyon Yes.

Harry What dissertation?

Lyon About the group. I've written the whole thing up. An account of the training programme. Everything. I think they found it really impressive. I really owe you guys.

Oliver I didn't know you were writing a dissertation.

Lyon Well, it's terribly dry. More of an academic manifesto, really.

Oliver So you'll be leaving.

Lyon Well, yes. But not till September. Sorry – I'm still reeling from the news.

Young Lad Have some sherry.

Lyon Thank you.

George Well, congratulations.

Jimmy So you're saying it was us that got you the job?

Lyon In a manner of speaking.

Susan Mr Lyon is a fantastic artist, though. Didn't you do something at the Essex Town Hall?

Oliver But what about the group?

Lyon You'll be fine. You're flying now. We'll get someone else for you.

Oliver But you don't understand. We rely on you for everything, Mr Lyon. That's what makes it work.

Lyon Oh, nonsense, Oliver. You make it work. I almost feel guilty about the dissertation. So much of it was you, really.

Oliver But you see things we can't. I thought you said it was a special relationship.

Lyon Well, it is a special relationship. And believe me, I won't let you down. I'll be back and forward anyway. You'll hardly notice I was gone.

George By rights you should have told us you were applying for another job.

Lyon I thought there was such a small chance of getting it, it was hardly worth bringing it up. I'm sorry, I'm hogging this whole thing.

Young Lad Don't be daft, it's fantastic.

Lyon Look. I know this is hardly the time for speeches but I just want to say, meeting you chaps, and the work we've done together over the last five years, is without a doubt the most profound, important and meaningful work – and beyond work, really – it's the most important thing that has ever happened to me. Coming up to Ashington, working shoulder to shoulder with you people. Of all the students I've taught, of all the great artists I've befriended . . . You chaps, your intelligence, your passion, your commitment, have made me feel humble on so many occassions. I know I will never find anything like this again. Really. Here's to the Group.

A siren starts. He looks askance.

Harry Oh, shit.

Jimmy You go for the rest of the sandwiches. I'll make a grab for the boiled ham.

The stage is bare. Lyon brings on an easel. Right at the back Oliver is behind a screen:

EDINBURGH COLLEGE OF ART, 1944

Lyon has set up an easel and is painting Oliver.

Oliver You do realise we would never wear any of this?

Lyon I thought this was a full pitman's uniform?

Oliver Well, maybes in 1790. You wouldn't wear all this now.

Lyon Why ever not?

Oliver It's too hot.

Lyon Hot?

Oliver At the moment I divvint really wear owt. A pair of hoggers – but if you went down there in this lot you wouldn't last ten minutes.

Lyon Stand still.

Oliver I think you'd only ever see folk wearing this in pictures.

Lyon draws. Standing awkwardly, Oliver holds still.

Lyon How is everything in Ashington?

Oliver It's not been so good, really. We meet when we can, but – it's not the same. You know they requisitioned the hut? To be quite honest we were ganna pack it in.

Lyon Pack it in?!

Oliver It's been really difficult since the news came about the young lad. George's been really knocked sideways by it. Admittedly Harry's a bit happier since Stalin's on the right side, but it's been tough.

Lyon I'm sorry.

Oliver It's not been easy for anyone. You should come down and see us.

Lyon I'll write to George as soon as term starts and I have my timetable. I can't believe it's been more than a year. I feel dreadful. I've been meaning to arrange something for months but – you know how things are.

Oliver The lads'd be very glad to see you.

Lyon I'll make it an absolute priority, I promise.

Oliver It's all right. I understand.

Lyon No, it's unforgivable. But I'll make up for it. (*Concentrating on the picture.*) Yes, very good. That's it. Don't move.

Oliver How are you getting on up here?

Lyon Rather well, as a matter of fact. It's so different actually being in a capital city. You know, with a real cultural life going on around you. Artists, writers, interesting people. A world away from the deserts of Jesmond. And the remarkable thing is, as part of my duties I have the responsibility for hanging the National Gallery of Scotland.

Oliver Really?

Lyon Absolutely thrilling. I had no idea.

Oliver What are you going to show next?

Lyon Well, actually, I was hoping to show you.

Oliver Me?!

Lyon Yes. Well, and the group, of course.

Oliver Yes, of course.

Lyon What do you think?

Oliver I don't know what to say – that's amazing.

Lyon No.

Oliver What a privilege.

Lyon Yes. Well, all of the permanent art's been moved to storage – for safe-keeping. So there are just a load of empty walls. And I thought of you.

Oliver 'Cos we won't get bombed.

Lyon We could any of us get bombed. I thought you'd be less precious. It just seemed like a real opportunity. I'd really love people up here to see what I've been up to. It's really important work, Oliver.

Oliver Well, I'll talk to the lads, then.

Lyon Please – it would mean a lot to me. To be totally honest, I feel terrible. I know I should have kept in touch. I'm perfectly aware that you felt that somehow I'd exploited the group. But you are incredibly important to me. You know that.

Oliver I don't think you exploited us. I owe you everything, Mr Lyon. I miss you a great deal.

Lyon Really?

Oliver Of course.

Lyon I didn't think you'd give me much thought.

Oliver No. You mean a great deal to me. It's just our circumstances are rather different, aren't they? How you getting on?

Oliver comes round. He looks at it.

Lyon Well, it's a start. Do you like it?

Oliver Yes. It's very . . . It's good.

Lyon Please. Have I taught you anything? Tell me what you think.

Oliver Really. I think it's good.

Lyon Don't be polite, Oliver. Come on. Tell me what you really think.

Oliver You know it's good. You don't need to hear what I've got to say.

Lyon Of course I do. Tell me what you think?

Oliver The truth? It's a perfectly fine academic study. An exercise well executed. As a piece of art, though – there's not a lot here. It's flat – superficial.

Lyon I see.

Oliver You've smoothed everything out, in a sort of 'idea' of a realistic, 'photographic' realism. If you look at all this light and shade – it's not actually realistic at all. I didn't look like that in the light. This is a stylised, generic representation – yes, there is some accuracy in recording my features but . . . Like a bit of a party trick – there's no real life in it.

Lyon Well . . .

Lyon starts to respond, but Oliver is not finished.

Oliver But if you really want to know what I think is wrong with the picture – it's that it fails to give any sense at all of what it meant to draw it. It doesn't give any sense of what I mean to you, what it might mean to be a pitman – to wear those clothes, to have me in your room, to be drawn – anything. It's bland – I think the word is 'facile'. That's a word, isn't it?

Lyon 'Facile'?

Oliver Yes. Full of facility but signifying nothing. Well, very little. I could be anyone. I'm not anyone, Mr Lyon.

Lyon I know you're not, Oliver.

Oliver Should I go on?

Lyon Please spare me the finer details. You're completely right. I know what this work is. I know what I am. I know I'm a failure in any real artistic sense. I don't have a subject. But this is what I do, this is who I am.

Oliver You're not a failure, Mr Lyon. You are everything I would have liked to have been.

Lyon Thank God you were saved that privilege.

Oliver Privilege? I'm not privileged, Mr Lyon, I am a miner. I work down there on my hands and knees forty-eight hours a week. Look at my hands. Look at your hands. I should be here. I should be doing what you do. I know I'm no great shakes, I know by any real standards I'm just as mediocre as you are – we're both in the same boat here. But I should be where you are. An important man, devoting all my time to art and literature and meeting brilliant people. Why can't that be me? I'm a miner, Mr Lyon. I might be proud, I might be independent. But we're not privileged in any way.

Lyon Rubbish, Oliver. You know and I know what matters is the art. When everybody's forgotten I ever exisited they'll be building galleries to show your work. That is the privilege. You got the gift. Everybody runs up against indifference, their limitations. That's the whole point of art – if it was easy it wouldn't mean anything. Yes, the world is unfair. Yes, other people have it easy. Well, go out and change it, Oliver. Use your anger.

Oliver I'm disappointed. I'm not angry.

Lyon Well, you bloody well should be. The point is, we can make a world where everyone can flourish. But you can't just do that by making art. Painting pictures by itself isn't going to change the world. What the hell did you think I was trying to do, coming up to Ashington? Art isn't enough by itself. You have to go into the world and change it. Don't you see? When this war is over there's a chance that we can actually do something, but it can only happen if the working classes get off their fat arses and fucking high horses and use their power, their intelligence and their creativity, Oliver, and reach for a better world. If they give up and accept the scraps thrown to them we're all fucked. You can't have a rich culture if three-quarters of the people are disenfranchised.

Listen, I was in the trenches, I saw then where I came from, that right beside me was a class of people who'd had none of the opportunities I had. Well, I came out and I've tried to make a difference. I might have failed, but it's different now – we fought another war. We cannot go back to the nineteen-thirties. We're on the brink here. Stop being scared of the world, Oliver. Meet it. Yes. The world is unjust. But we can change this country – not just a little bit, but we can change it fundamentally. Be brave. Take your chances. Make something new.

They look at one another.

Footage: photographs of the war; archive photos of bombing in Newcastle and Ashington; Germans on the retreat; the 1945 election; nationalisation of the coal industry.

1947
THE HUT — EVE OF NATIONALISATION

George is up a ladder hammering in a sign. Jimmy is holding the ladder.

Jimmy I divvint knaa why you're putting this up in the first place.

George To celebrate getting the hut back. Ne WEA, ne Robert Lyon, ne borrowing stuff off the Scouts. This is wor hut – we're the bosses now.

Jimmy I still divvint see what we need all these rules for.

George Well, you've got to have rules. Else it'd be bloody anarchy wi yous lot. Anyway, this is just the principles, there's a special book coming with the entire constitution.

Harry comes in.

Harry What ye deing?

George What's it look like? I'm putting up the rules.

Harry What do we need rules for?

George Look, divvint you start or I'll put you on probation.

Harry You can't do that.

George Can't I now? Article 15, Section c. You watch yerself.

Harry (*looking round*) It's not too bad, is it?

Jimmy And it's got electricity. Thanks to the conscientious objector.

116

Harry Aye, he was a nice lad – for a boss's son.

George He wasn't that conscientious, I nearly electrocuted meself on that fuse box. Anyway, I think we've done all right, getting a permanent lease off the Coal Board – despite the electrical inadequacies.

Harry They had ne choice – now they're a nationalised industry.

George There was a lot of competition from Amateur Dramatics. Turns oot every bugger's an artist under Clement Attlee.

Jimmy Still ten shillings a years, not nowt, ye knaa.

George But just you wait till the new subscriptions start coming in. This place'll be heaving.

Harry What's that racket?

George It's the band next door. They're practising for the Picnic.

Jimmy It'll be a hell of a do this year.

George Aye, all change. I never thought I'd see it in my lifetime.

Harry Ye of little faith.

George Do yous fancy a bottle of beer?

Jimmy You don't drink, George.

George I knaa, but it's a special occasion. It's from that lad, remember. Here. Just this once to celebrate.

Jimmy I divvint knaa aboot celebrating. It took a bloody war to make this possible.

Harry It was inevitable.

Jimmy Inevitable?

Harry The inexorable rise of the working classes, comrade. Give uz one.

George Wey, it's all ganna change now.

Harry And this is just the start. You wait till the Health Service kicks in. Education, the railways. It's ganna be a completely different world, man.

Jimmy Divvint get yer hopes up. Labour?! They'll sell wi down the river just like the last time.

George They've got to do it. They've got no choice with this mandate. There.

Harry Look at the state of that. How do you expect to inaugurate the road to socialism if you can't even put up a sign straight?

Oliver comes in.

Oliver Give uz a hand.

George What the hell's that?

Oliver Careful. Here – put it down.

Harry What is it?

Oliver I decided I should do something useful for a change. What yous deing?

Jimmy We're having a beer.

Oliver But yous divvint drink.

George Well, we are today, it's a special occasion. Have one.

Oliver Well, howay, help uz open it. I've been painting it all weekend up at the Mechanics' Hall. I've been thinking, maybes Harry's reet, maybes we should be doing something more political.

They unfurl it. It is the banner that he's drawn.

Jimmy It's a banner.

George I can see it's a bleeding banner.

Oliver On the back there's a picture of how it is now. And this is the front.

Harry 'Forward to Socialism'.

Oliver It's a sort of allegory. That was the past. This is the future.

George That's not an allegory.

Oliver What you talking about?

George An allegory is a figurative mode of representation containing a meaning other than the literal. That is a literal depiction.

Jimmy It can't be that literal – I didn't even recognise it.

Oliver Of course you didn't recognise it. It's how it will be. That's why it's allegorical.

Jimmy I wouldn't want my windows that colour.

Oliver It doesn't matter about the colour. The point is the message.

Jimmy What message?

Oliver Closing the door on the past.

Jimmy I quite like the past.

Oliver I mean poverty, misery, exploitation.

Harry Are you feeling all right, Oliver?

Oliver What's wrong with being against poverty, misery and exploitation?

Harry Nothing at all, Oliver. Nothing at all.

Oliver Well, what do you think?

Jimmy It's very canny, aye.

Oliver But as a concept?

Harry It's very good. Very clear, Oliver.

Oliver It's obviously a different sort of statement than the usual banner. You know, ne Karl Marx or Arthur Cook. I thought it should be something normal – something we can connect to.

Jimmy I divvint knaa. You could put Keir Hardie up at that window.

George Shut it, Jimmy.

Oliver Do you think it works?

Harry As a banner?

Oliver As art?

Harry To be quite honest, as art it works better as a banner.

Oliver I thought you'd like the message, Harry.

Harry I do. I'm not sure I like the painting.

Jimmy What's wrang with it?

Harry It doesn't seem like one of yours.

Oliver What do you mean?

Harry There are no people in it, Oliver.

Oliver Bloody hell. You're right. I thought there was something wrong with it.

Harry What's the point of Utopia with nebody in it?

Jimmy That's alreet, you could put a few fellas in by that tree.

Harry No – you should leave it. It is what it is. It's a perfectly good banner.

Oliver I just thought it was a way forward. A way of using wer art, like.

George Making banners?

Oliver Doing something useful.

Harry Listen, plenty of people can paint banners, Oliver. But nebody's deing what we de.

Oliver What do we do?

Harry We make wor life art. It doesn't get better than that. Nebody telling us what to paint. No master but ourselves.

Oliver But surely it matters what we paint.

Harry Yes. And what do we paint, Oliver? Moments. We paint those little, tiny moments of being alive. Of life passing by. Tiny things in the corner of an eye. The things nebody else will paint. Moments. That's what life really is. Very rarely do big things happen – life is all this stuff, all these little things which are lost in a moment if somebody doesn't get them down. This is what living is, that's what we paint; the fall of light – the magic of being alive – and nebody else'll do it. If we divvint get it down, it's all gone.

It's like in Marx, you mine in the morning, swim in the afternoon and make art at night. That's how it should be. That's how your folk songs are written and yer cathedrals were made. And what we've done is to do it together. It's not about what you do, Oliver, or I do, or Jimmy, or how good it is, it's that we've done this together as a group. The value of art isn't in one bit – you divvint look in the corner of the *Mona Lisa* for the meaning – the value of art is in the 'whole'. It's all of this, this is what we've made.

And nobody told us to paint them, nobody paid us to do this. This is us. This is our lives. Sod it if we're not fashionable – who cares who criticises wi? 'Cos we're not deing it for anybody else, we're deing for worselves; and sod it, it's more than that – we're doing it for all those lives in the dark, who never had the chance. For the thousands of little pit laddies without an education, the blokes with their backs bent and their hands busted open – folk who've barely got the energy to get home, never mind to start deing art when they get there. We're deing it for all of those lives unrecorded. All of that creativity unfulfilled. That's why we should be proud and that's what we will continue doing: making our lives art because we are alive, here and now. (*Pause.*) End of lecture.

George Hear, hear. And we're still here through thick and thin.

Oliver True. Look, if this is what we managed to achieve wi nowt, just think of what we'll be to achieve in the future.

George Nebody's ganna be satisfied with just coming off their shift and vegetating – they're all ganna want what we want. For centuries and centuries they kept aal the good stuff for themselves. But they're not ganna leave yer Shakespeare and Goethe just for the upper classes now – it's ganna belang to us.

Harry This is just the start. This place'll be an academy. In years to come it'll be teeming with artists in here: bakers, pitmen, housewives –

George Steady on, Harry.

Harry Everybody actually living a proper creative life.

George Not about consuming the rubbish they flog to you. Scraps off the table.

Oliver No, making something for worselves.

George The University of Ashington. There'll be pitmen poets and pitmen painters –

Harry – with PhDs, there'll be pitmen professors, the lot.

George Actually, that's a contradiction in terms. I knaa thousands have died and I knaa it was hell, but it's ganna be worth it. All change.

Jimmy The working classes are coming to get ye.

Oliver To the future –

George To nationalisation –

Oliver And absent friends.

Harry To the National Health Service –

George Dental care for all.

Jimmy To culture.

George To the common man –

Harry And aspiration –

George Aye, aspiration.

Oliver And socialism –

Jimmy And socialism.

Harry And art –

Jimmy And art –

George – of the people –

Jimmy – to the people.

Oliver With plenty people in it.

Harry Hear, hear.

Jimmy Listen, they've got it.

Oliver 'Gresford'.

The music from next door wells up. The guys listen.

George It's beautiful.

*They listen to it: it is beautiful, stirring. One of them
starts singing and after a few lines gradually all join
in, rising to the end of a verse.*

All
Lord of the oceans and the sky above,
Whose wondrous grace has blessed us from our birth,
Look with compassion, and with love
On all who toil beneath the earth.

They spend their lives in dark, with danger fraught,
Remote from nature's beauties, far below,
Winning the coal, oft dearly bought
To drive the wheel, the hearth make glow.

*The loud sound of a buzzer breaks them off.
Blackout.*

Projection:

NO UNIVERSITY OF ASHINGTON
WAS FOUNDED

WOODHORN COLLIERY
WAS CLOSED IN 1981

IN 1995, THE CALL FOR THE
'COMMON OWNERSHIP OF
THE MEANS OF PRODUCTION,
DISTRIBUTION AND EXCHANGE'
WAS EXCISED FROM THE
LABOUR PARTY CONSTITUTION